RIEL

RIEL

a play in two parts by
JOHN COULTER

CROMLECH PRESS, HAMILTON, ONTARIO • 1972

For
my daughter
C L A R E
whose passion is theatre

Designed by Carl Dair, F.T.D.C.

R I E L THIS PLAY IN TWO PARTS is designed for presentation in the Elizabethan manner: a continuous flow of scenes on a bare stage with the aid of no more than indicative settings and properties and modern stage lighting.

Of the numerous persons who appear, few of those in Part One are seen again in Part Two, and some of those appearances are brief and do not recur. Hence, with actors doubling their roles, a cast of twenty-five is sufficient for all speaking parts. Non-speaking parts for crowd scenes may be cast to whatever extent the resources of a production allow.

The action takes place in the North-West Territories, now part of Canada, during the seventies and eighties of the last century.

PART ONE 1869-1870

1. *Riel's Living Room*
2. *River Meadows near Fort Garry*
3. *Room in Fort Garry*
4. *Fort Garry Precincts*
5. *Cell in Fort Garry*
6. *Room in Fort Garry*
7. *An Open Place in Ontario*
8. *Fort Garry Precincts*
9. *Prime Minister's Room, Ottawa*
10. *Fort Garry Precincts*
11. *Room in Fort Garry*
12. *Room in Fort Garry*

PART TWO 1885-1886

1. *Porch of Riel's House, Montana*
2. *An Open Place in Saskatchewan*
3. *Another Open Place in Saskatchewan*
4. *Church at Batoche*
5. *Outside Riel's House, Batoche*
6. *Tent of General Middleton*
7. *Courtroom, Regina*
8. *Vicinity of Courtroom, Regina*
9. *Courtroom, Regina*
10. *Vicinity of Courtroom, Regina*
11. *Courtroom, Regina*
12. *Corridor to Cells in Police Barracks, Regina*
13. *Cell in Police Barracks, Regina*
14. *Precincts of Parliament, Ottawa*
15. *Prime Minister's Room, Ottawa*
16. *Precincts of Police Barracks, Regina*
17. *Cell and Precincts in Police Barracks, Regina*
18. *A Place of Prayer and Mourning*

THE PERSONS: *In Part One and Part Two*

RIEL   *Louis Riel, leader of the Métis, the half-breeds*

MOTHER   *His mother, a white woman*

MACDONALD   *Sir John A. Macdonald, Prime Minister of Canada*

In Part One Only

PRIEST   *A local curé*

RABBIE   *Scots settler*

XAVIER   *Half-breed*

FRANCOIS   *Half-breed*

SCOTT   *Thomas Scott, navvy, Orangeman from Ontario*

DENNIS   *Colonel Stoughton Dennis, surveyor*

O'DONOGHUE   *One of the Council, a Fenian*

YOUNG   *Methodist minister*

SMITH   *Donald A. Smith, later Lord Strathcona*

TACHE   *Bishop of St. Boniface*

WOLSELEY   *Colonel Garnet Wolseley*

CARTIER   *Sir Georges Etienne Cartier*

SERGEANT   *British regular*

SURVEYORS, VOLUNTEER SETTLERS, HALF-BREEDS, INDIANS

In Part Two Only

MARGUERITE   *Indian wife of Riel*

INDIAN   *Riel partisan*

HALF-BREED   *Riel partisan*

PRIEST   *A local curé*

WOMAN	*Half-breed*
ARMSTRONG	*Scout, with Middleton's forces*
MIDDLETON	*General Frederick Middleton*
CLERK	*Clerk of the Court*
JUDGE	*His Honour Judge Richardson*
CROWN	*Counsel for the Crown*
DEFENCE	*Counsel for the Defence*
NOLIN	*Charles Nolin, cousin of Riel*
ANDRE	*Father Alexis André*
ROY	*Dr. Francis Roy*
JUKES	*Dr. Jukes, police surgeon*
POLICEMAN	*North-West Mounted Police Officer*
SHERIFF	*Deputy Sheriff Gibson*
MARC	*Newspaperman*
BILL	*Newspaperman*
FOREMAN	*Foreman of the jury*
CHAPLEAU	*Hon. J. A. Chapleau*
TROOPER	*Another North-West Mounted Police Officer*

FATHER MCWILLIAMS, HANGMAN, PEOPLE

RIEL: PART ONE

SCENE 1 *Riel's Living Room*

A table. Some chairs. Lamplight. The living-room of Riel's house near Fort Garry. PRIEST *and* O'DONOGHUE *are waiting with the half-breeds* FRANCOIS *and* XAVIER. *Except for the* PRIEST, *they are wearing bandoliers and have Enfield rifles. Riel's* MOTHER, *a brooding, watchful, raw-boned woman of the frontier, is also present.*

FRANCOIS

We wait. We wait. He does not come.

XAVIER

Always it is like this. But if he does not come soon. . . .

MOTHER

He will come when it is time to come.

O'DONOGHUE

The time to come was an hour ago. What right has he to keep us waiting here twirling our thumbs?

MOTHER

Always when he must decide something, he goes riding on the plains. . . .

O'DONOGHUE

His solitary pow-wows with the Almighty! So he can blame his unpunctuality on the Almighty—who's always punctual himself or what a divil of a smash-up there'd be in his universe!

PRIEST

Mr. O'Donoghue, in my presence at least if you would refrain from trifling with the attributes of the Almighty.

O'DONOGHUE

Is it trifling, to wish that a touch of the divine attribute
of absolute punctuality should be acquired by Riel. . . ?

[*He is interrupted by the entrance
of* RABBIE, *a Scots settler, who also has
bandolier and rifle.*]

MOTHER

Rabbie, Rabbie, he comes, my Louis? He comes now?

RABBIE

Naw, not yet. No sign o' him yet. The laddies are
gathering at the rendezvous frae all airts and pairts,
but no sign of him. Ambroise Lepine is there. *Adjutant*
Lepine, beg pardon.

FRANCOIS

Ambroise! [*Hurriedly rising.*] It is time we go.

XAVIER

Ya! *He* gets mad always if *we* are late!

MOTHER

Go then, François. Go Xavier.

RABBIE

Aye, it'll be "Fall in!" by the time we get the length.
Are you coming with us or biding, Mr. O'Donoghue?

O'DONOGHUE

I'll be after you.

MOTHER

I will go where I think Louis is. I will bring him.

[MOTHER *goes out
with* RABBIE, FRANCOIS *and*
XAVIER.]

PRIEST

Mr. O'Donoghue. You're one of the few men of education here. I must appeal to you. If you would help to
restrain this madness. . . .

O'DONOGHUE

But father, I'm the maddest of the mad myself—if any
of us *are* mad! I disagree with Riel. But chiefly because
his madness isn't mad enough. He's for holding the
North-West—but under protection of the British flag.
I'm for holding it under the protection of our own
flag, our own arms!

PRIEST

I had hoped that even at this last moment common
sense and Christian teaching might prevail.

O'DONOGHUE

It's common sense and Christian teaching to fight off any attempt by an invader to march in. . . . Or what do you want us to do? Run out and welcome the invader? Fire a salute! Send an escort!

PRIEST

It's ridiculous to speak of the survey-party sent here by the Canadian government as invaders.

O'DONOGHUE

They're the vanguard of the invasion.

PRIEST

Nonsense.

O'DONOGHUE

If we tolerate them Canadians will swarm in after them in thousands. They'll grab both us and ours. They'll lay us under tribute. Tax us! Bleed us white! For what? To help them build great buildings and roads and bridges and railways and canals—but not here! Not for us in the North-West. No, but for themselves, in Canada! To make their own big cities bigger and richer still! But no, oh no! We won't let Canada do to us what England did to Ireland. . . .

PRIEST

There we go! There we go! The thorn in the flesh for ever!

O'DONOGHUE

What any big over-blown nation in history does to a small neighbour—grab it! Gobble it up!

PRIEST

Your Irish eloquence runs away with you.

O'DONOGHUE

Irish eloquence is the flame leaping out of the fire— the passion for the rights of small peoples.

PRIEST

Yes, yes, but as well as flame there is also much smoke. It may blind you to the long perspectives, the larger purpose of Providence for *all* peoples.

O'DONOGHUE

Meaning what?

PRIEST

Meaning that history must unfold according to the divine plan in the mind of God. Whoever or whatever tries to stop it will be broken.

Meaning Riel and the rest of us here, the Council, will be broken?

PRIEST

Yes. If what you persist in doing is contrary to the divine plan.

O'DONOGHUE

As God won't take us into his confidence about his plan we must go on and risk being broken, if necessary, for what we think is right.

PRIEST

And who will decide what is to be thought right?

O'DONOGHUE

Ah! Now *that's* a question! But here's the oracle. Ask him.

> [RIEL *has come in with his* MOTHER. RIEL *is an intense young man in his mid-twenties. He has some Indian blood. He has a moustache and sideburns. He wears a tweed jacket with dark trousers and moccasins. He does not carry arms, nor consequently does he wear a bandolier. He has on a woollen toque. He bows deeply to the priest and nods to* O'DONOGHUE.]

PRIEST

Monsieur Riel!

O'DONOGHUE

If you'll excuse me, I'll join my comrades in arms.

> [O'DONOGHUE *goes out.*]

PRIEST

An unbeliever.

RIEL

But a good accountant. We will use him in our Provisional Government.

PRIEST

Louis Riel, I am your friend as well as your priest. As your friend I warn you: this step you and the Council are taking—it is bound to have the most serious consequences.

RIEL

We have weighed the consequences, father. We must go on.

PRIEST

And if you fail?

RIEL

We will not fail.

PRIEST

But suppose—*suppose* you do?

RIEL

Suppose? No. It is no good to suppose what must not be.

PRIEST

In any case, passions will be let loose. There's bound to be killing: much bloodshed and great misery.

RIEL

We will do all we can to avoid bloodshed.

PRIEST

You won't succeed. You can't.

RIEL

I think we may.

PRIEST

No.

RIEL

Well, that is your opinion.

PRIEST

My opinion. Having given it, as emphatically and plainly as I can, I don't feel I can do more. It is a matter outside my province as a priest.

RIEL

Yes, father, yes. Outside your province. [*With point.*] It is good that you see this.

PRIEST

[*Nettled.*] *You* tell *me* what is good!

RIEL

I think it is God's will that we . . . .

PRIEST

You tell *me* what is God's will!

RIEL

I have prayed much. I have asked God. I think God is with us.

PRIEST

I've heard you speak in this manner before. Presuming to know the mind of God. This grows on you. I have warned you it is a fearful presumption, particularly in a layman.

RIEL

God has made his will known to laymen before.

PRIEST

God speaks through Holy Church.

RIEL

But father, I am a member of Holy Church, humble and obedient.

PRIEST

In some things about as humble and obedient as Lucifer.

MOTHER

No father, no, do not say this. . . .

RIEL

That will do, that will do! [*To* PRIEST, *rising to end the discussion.*] I think there is nothing more to say.

PRIEST

[*Not accepting it.*] Even that is for you to decide!

RIEL

Father I have heard your opinion.

PRIEST

Only to disregard it. A whole community is to be plunged in bloodshed simply because you say so.

RIEL

The people and the Council say so.

PRIEST

Persuaded by you. What will they say when precious lives have been lost and we are mourning our dead?

RIEL

God will give us the victory.

PRIEST

So that you may set yourself up to lord it over everyone with the high hand!

RIEL

You must not say this!

[*Exclamation from* MOTHER.]

PRIEST

But if instead you find yourself before a firing squad. . . .

MOTHER

Oh father!

PRIEST

Do not blame it on God or the people. It will be your own fault.

RIEL

My fault, my fault.

PRIEST

For the last time I must admonish you. . . .

RIEL

Not again please. You will not.

PRIEST

I am not asking your permission.

RIEL

Father, I will continue to make my confession to you as my priest, humbly and penitently. But you will not over-rule me in what as you say is outside your province. That is all. Now shall we leave this? I will pray for you, father. Will you please pray for me?

PRIEST

As I pray for all the insolent and erring.

RIEL

Pray that I may be kept humble and faithful.

PRIEST

Oh Louis, Louis, if only you could acquire a little, even a little genuine humility.

RIEL

I will try, father.

[*The tramping of men not properly trained to march is heard, coming nearer.*]

MOTHER

There! They are riding!

RIEL

The volunteers.

PRIEST

Then it is too late, for anything but prayer. . . [*Voice of command, off. The troop halts.*] and pained disapproval of—mock soldiering.

RIEL

Mock soldiering!

MOTHER

They have Enfield rifles, father, every man. And fifty rounds.

PRIEST

You seem well-versed in the particulars.

RIEL

From tonight they will enforce our authority here, our Provisional Government. . . .

PRIEST

[*Preparing to leave.*] My coming has been a waste of time.

RIEL

Not altogether. I wanted to see you, to ask you something. [*The* PRIEST *waits to hear.*] We have appointed you chaplain.

PRIEST

Chaplain?

RIEL

To our Catholic volunteers.

PRIEST

Your Catholic volunteers! Do you mean my parishioners?

RIEL

Most of them, yes. You will be chaplain?

PRIEST

Chaplain nonsense! They're my parishioners. Whatever folly you and the Council may lead them into I will still attend to their spiritual needs.

RIEL

That is all we ask.

PRIEST

Your asking has nothing to do with it.

RIEL

No, father, no. I thank you. [*The* PRIEST *is again turning to leave.*] Before you go, father. Will you bless me now? [*Kneels.*]

MOTHER

[*Also kneeling.*] And me, father.

PRIEST

[*To Riel.*] Certainly not as leader of this—insurrection.

RIEL

No, father, only as the most humble, most unworthy of your parishioners.

PRIEST

May God in his mercy help you to become truly humble and less unworthy. [*Signing them with the cross as he gives the blessing.*] Benedictio Dei omnipotentis patris et filii et spiritus sancti descendat super vos et maneat semper. Amen.

RIEL and MOTHER

Amen.

PRIEST

[*Quietly, in paternal affection.*] Oh Louis, Louis Riel, what *am* I to make of you?

SCENE 2   *River Meadows near Fort Garry*

*The river-meadows near Fort Garry. Bright morning.
A hullabaloo of angry, protesting voices is heard
approaching from the right. Presently the incensed
people, half-breeds, settlers, an Indian — come in,
gesticulating and looking off left towards the occasion
of the trouble. Most of the men are volunteers. They
are armed with rifles and wear bandoliers, but they
are in their working clothes and farm boots or moccasins. Among them are:* RABBIE, *the Scots settler who,
for this occasion, may be wearing his kilts and tam-o-
shanter;* FRANÇOIS *and* XAVIER, *the two French-Indian
half-breeds or Métis. Riel's* MOTHER.

RABBIE

[*In Scots accent.*] Grabbers! Land grabbers! That's
what they are!

> [CAST: *ad lib.: "Oui Oui!
> Aye! Grabbers! Land
> Grabbers."*]

RABBIE

Surveyors they call themselves. But they're here to
grab our lands! Look at them! Measuring!

XAVIER

[*Very agitated.*] That is my field they measure now!
First, André Nault's. Now, mine! They go there. They
measure! They do not ask! [*Putting up rifle and sight-
ing as if to fire.*] Ah, they will not! they will not!

MOTHER

[*Pulling down the rifle.*] Wait, Xavier. Wait for Louis.

RABBIE

Aye, dinna fash yoursels, lads. You'll laugh when you
see them scootin' back hame to the East wi' their tails
atween their legs—an' a pickle or two o' lead in their
behinds for auld lang syne.

XAVIER

We take them prisoners.

FRANCOIS

Ya, ya, prisoners.

[Other approving "ya ya's."
A move in the direction off left
is checked by Riel's MOTHER.]

MOTHER

Wait for Louis. Let Louis deal with them.

[From up left, a road-navvy has come in and
witnessed the action. He carries a shovel or some
other implement indicative of his trade. He
wears working clothes, and is a surly, aggressive,
fanatical-looking man. This is THOMAS SCOTT.]

SCOTT

What's up here, folks, yous wi' your guns an' all?
[Catching at one of the rifles and then at one of the
bandoliers in a contemptuous, inquisitive way.]
Enfields, no less! And cartridges! Who might yous be
for shootin' at?

RABBIE

Maybe yoursel'.

SCOTT

Eh!

RABBIE

If you dinna march on an quit pokin' your long Ulster
snout in what disna concern you.

SCOTT

[With slow provocativeness.] Frae Scotlan', eh! *[If*
Rabbie is wearing kilts.] Kilts an' all, eh!

RABBIE

[Very angry.] March on, Ah tell you.

SCOTT

Man oh man oh man! And who do you think you're
givin' orders to, you funny wee kiltie you!

RABBIE

[Cocking the rifle.] Mind yoursel' now or I'll gie you
what you're workin' for.

SCOTT

You would would you! [*Grabs at the rifle.*] Gimme that gun here.

RABBIE

If you dare lay hand on it!

MOTHER

No, Rabbie, no, it is enough. [*Turning on* SCOTT.] And you. Go on you. Go. [*She pushes him.*]

SCOTT

Mind who you're pushin' missus.

FRANCOIS

We know.

XAVIER

Ya.

FRANCOIS

Thomas Scott.

SCOTT

That's right.

FRANCOIS

Orangeman. From Ontario.

SCOTT

Right again. Yous is all Catholics I suppose.

MOTHER

We do not want Orangemen here. Go on. Go!

> [*Others join in with:*
> "*Go on. Go!*"]

SCOTT

I'll go when I'm ready to go and not till then. And I'm takin' no orders from a pack o' mongrel Papishes.

> [*This provokes an outraged chorus of:*
> "*Mongrel! Papishes!*" *The half-breeds and*
> *the Indian move threateningly on* SCOTT
> *with:* "*Kill him! Kill him!*"]

SCOTT

[*Throwing away his shovel or implement and circling away from them with his fists raised.*] Try it on, then, try it on, till I beat the gizzards out o' yous. Come on. [*Throws off his coat.*] Who's first for the massacree? I'll beat the best man o' the lot o' yous so come on the first o' yous that wants a lump o' his death. [*Selects* FRANCOIS.] You there, Frenchie. I'll fight you first. Come on, if you're a proper fightin' man and not a Papish mongrel and a coward born. [*Strikes him.*] There's your cowardy.

FRANCOIS

[*Leaping at him.*] Coward! He calls me coward!

XAVIER

[*And others.*] Kill him! Kill him, François!

MOTHER

[*Trying to get him away.*] No no, François. The mad
Orange dog . . . . [*Turning to the right as she fails to
stop them.*] Oh where is Louis! Come, Louis, come!
[*Hurries off down right to fetch him.*]

SCOTT

One of yous at a time. One of yous at a time and I'll
beat the gizzards out o' the whole jing-bang o' yous.

[*While the scuffle is at its height, with* SCOTT
and FRANCOIS *flailing at each other, and the
others encouraging* FRANCOIS *excitedly, two
members of a survey party hurry in from up
left. Although they resemble English sportsmen,
they are, in fact, from Ontario. They are*
COLONEL STOUGHTON DENNIS *and* MR. WEBB.
They vigorously intervene.]

DENNIS

Look here, look here you people you can't do this.
[*Between them.*] Drop it. Drop it I say. [*Pushing*
FRANCOIS *towards his friends to the right.*] Keep that
man back. [*With* WEBB's *help pushing* SCOTT *to the
left.*] Keep away you. Calm yourself. Control yourself.

SCOTT

Papish mongrels! Cowards born!

DENNIS

Calm down. Restrain yourself.

SCOTT

I'll smoflicate the whole jing-bang o' them, aye be
Jasus will I and with one hand tied behind my back.
Let me at them. Let me at them.

DENNIS

Be on your way. Go on. Take yourself off!

SCOTT

Holy kripes! So *yous* is for givin' me orders next!

DENNIS

Go on. You're making yourself obnoxious to the people
here.

SCOTT

And what about yous—land grabbers!

DENNIS

Land grabbers! Balderdash!

SCOTT

It's what *they* called yous. [*Shouts at group round* FRANCOIS *over to the right.*] Hi! Did yous call these ones [*Jerks his thumb at Dennis and Webb.*] land grabbers or did yous not?

DENNIS

[*Advancing to placate them.*] Please, please, never mind this man. I'm Colonel Dennis. Colonel Stoughton Dennis. Mr. Webb with me. Our party came out here from Ontario with full authority to make a survey. . . .

[*From the right.* RIEL *has come in quickly with his* MOTHER *and two armed half-breed guards. He has no rifle or bandolier. He at once intervenes.*]

RIEL

I beg your pardon Colonel Dennis. I am Louis Riel. I speak for the people here.

DENNIS

Indeed!

RIEL

You are not permitted to trespass any longer here.

DENNIS

Did you say trespass?

RIEL

These plains of the North-West are not for sale. Your survey will not be tolerated.

DENNIS

My dear man may I just say. . . .

RIEL

No.

DENNIS

I have a right to speak.

RIEL

Pardon, you have no rights whatever here.

DENNIS

These are the Queen's domains. We're British subjects. Canadian citizens.

SCOTT

[*Slapping* DENNIS *heartily on the back and being pushed angrily off by* DENNIS.] Bully Stoughty!

RIEL

Canadians have no rights whatever in these Territories.

SCOTT

Ach don't heed the Papish mongrel.

[*Outcries at this.*]

RIEL

[*To guards, sternly.*] If that man interrupts again, arrest him.

[SCOTT *advances menacingly on* RIEL, *and* RIEL'S MOTHER *and others move forward to intercept him. But* RIEL *holds up his hand to stop them. In tense silence, he stands quite still and eyes* SCOTT.]

SCOTT

Who do *you* think you are?

[*He suddenly strikes* RIEL. *In the same fraction of time the* GUARDS *pounce on him, and there are exclamations of shock and anger from all except* RIEL, *who stands rigid.*]

MOTHER

He is the devil. He is the devil!

RIEL

Take him away.

[SCOTT *is being subdued and dragged off to the left by the* GUARDS *with the assistance of* FRANCOIS *and* XAVIER, *who will return later.*]

SCOTT

[*As they struggle with him.*] Lemme go. Lemme go. Lemme go till I knock the stuffin' out o' yous.

DENNIS

Unforgivable. An obnoxious fanatic.

RIEL

He will be punished.

MOTHER

He is the devil, the devil. For this he should be shot.

RIEL

[*To* DENNIS.] As for you, please. You go back to Canada. At once. I order this.

DENNIS

Would you mind enlightening us—by what author-**ity.** . . .

RIEL

By authority of the Provisional Government we set up today.

DENNIS

I think you must be mad.

[*Exclamation from* MOTHER: *"Louis!"*]

RIEL

You are speaking to the representative of the Provisional Government.

DENNIS

The Hudson's Bay Company are the legal government here under charter from her Majesty.

RIEL

Not now. They traded or tried to trade these Territories and us that live on them to Canada—without consulting us. But we will not be bought and sold. Three hundred thousand pounds from Canada—to fill the pockets of the [*Bitterly contemptuous.*] Honourable Company of Gentlemen Adventurers. . . . A pretty mess of pottage for *our* birthright! [RIEL *shouts and he shakes his clenched fist.*] The Honourable Adventurers will not sit on their honourable backsides in London and sell *us*—to Canada, or any other bidder. Twelve thousand of us. . . .

DENNIS

[*Bored.*] I hate to interrupt but if you'll allow me. . . .

RIEL

Twelve thousand loyal subjects of her Majesty. We own these lands, these plains of the North-West are ours. We had them from our mothers who had them from God, our country since the beginning of the world. [*Again there are shouts.*] Are they such fools in London and Ottawa—to think we can be pushed about and spat upon—sold, like we were sheep—twelve thousand head of sheep!

[*There are cries of delighted approval from* RIEL's *supporters:* "Bravo!" "Vive!"]

MOTHER

Good, Louis! Good, good!

RABBIE

[*Simultaneously.*] Fine, Mister Riel, fine! Rub their noses in it man!

DENNIS

[*Wearily patient.*] Is it my turn now to say just a word?

RIEL

It is not a discussion. I tell what is happening here
and I am trying to be patient to tell it. . . .

DENNIS

Oh the dickens with it!

RIEL

Because it is important. It is a great important principle. The people of a country [*His voice rises towards
a passionate climax.*] can not be taken over and incor-
porated into some other country without their own
consent. To try to do that to a people is an outrage.
A violation of the rights and dignities of free men. We
will fight against it. God has directed me. . .

DENNIS

Suppose we leave God out of it.

MOTHER

To leave God out of it!

RIEL

In London and Ottawa you may leave God out of it
but we are Christians here [*He adds, with venom.*]
not savages.

DENNIS

Yes, yes, yes, but about your rights and dignities of
course they'll be respected by Canada.

RIEL

Of course for I will make sure, very sure—if I agree to
treat with Canada. . . .

DENNIS

If *you* agree.

RIEL

And if Canada accepts my terms. . . .

DENNIS

Your terms.

RIEL

To enter Confederation.

DENNIS

I think you're a preposterous, presumptuous fool, fit
only to be certified.

[*Bystanders are incensed. There are
shouts of: "Strike him." "Slap his mouth."
"Shoot him."*]

MOTHER

    He will not say this. Do not take this Louis.

RIEL

    [*With some irritation, quelling her and the others.*]
Please I will deal with it.

> [*As this is happening, another Scots
> SETTLER comes in, right—a farmer, carrying
> a rake or pitchfork. He halts and
> watches but takes no side. Meanwhile
> DENNIS and WEBB have turned away
> to go off to the left.*]

DENNIS

    Come on, Webb, enough of this tomfoolery.

> [*But at a sign from RIEL, XAVIER
> and FRANCOIS bar the way with
> their rifles cocked.*]

DENNIS

    Out of our way you scallywags.

RIEL

    [*To their backs, with cool politeness.*] Pardon, gentle-
men. If you please.

DENNIS

    [*Disregarding him.*] How dare you try to stop us.
Stand aside.

MOTHER

    [*Peremptorily.*] When Louis speaks, turn round!

RIEL

    [*To her, sharply.*] I can deal with it. [*To his back.*]
Colonel Dennis I wait.

> [*DENNIS and WEBB turn around from
> the levelled rifles reluctantly.*]

DENNIS

    Well, as you have the coward's advantage of us. . . .

RIEL

    You and your party will leave the settlement at once.
I give you twenty-four hours to be across the border.
After that if I catch any of you here. . . .

DENNIS

    Well, go on?

RIEL

    I think I will not catch you. But if I do you will be put
in irons and locked up. [*Pointing off, up left.*] There in
Fort Garry.

DENNIS

[*Surprised.*] Fort Garry?

RIEL

By noon we will have marched in. Some of us have already entered the gates.

DENNIS

Then I can only say if ever a dangerous irresponsible madman was at large I'm talking to him now. [*Turning to the others and stopping them as they begin to protest.*] As for you, you can't know what this means. I beg you don't let him lead you on, or you'll be parties to his criminal folly and you'll be crushed with him for crushed he'll surely be. There's still time to save yourselves. Which of you'll be the first?

[*The Scots* SETTLER, *who entered earlier, moves across to* DENNIS *who looks at* RIEL.]

DENNIS

Here's one who doesn't side with you. Any others? [*Singling them out.*] What about you? And you? [*They stare stonily back at him without moving.*]

RIEL

[*After a moment; smiling, ironic.*] What! No others! [*To* DENNIS.] You see. And everywhere it is the same. With all the people—all are with me but a few [*Glaring at* SETTLER.] traitors.

DENNIS

Whoever doesn't side with you's a traitor.

RIEL

Yes traitor—to the folks they made their home with here. [*His voice rises to a frenzy.*] But God's my witness if our traitors organize against us I will strike them down—without warning or mercy. I will seize their homes and fields and stock and arms and stores. I will batter them down—[*In a paroxysm.*] sweep them from this soil they desecrate.

[*A shocked silence. There is a shout, off to the left.* THOMAS SCOTT *rushes in wildly excited.*]

SCOTT

[*To* DENNIS *and* WEBB.] Hi, hi! What are yous waitin' for! Don't yous know what's afoot?

DENNIS

[*With distaste.*] Back again. You.

SCOTT

The heathen mongrels is marchin' down the road.
They're headin' for the Fort. Most o' them's half-roads
there already and some o' them's right inside the gates.
Come on, Colonel, give us our marchin' orders!

RIEL

[*To* XAVIER *and* FRANCOIS *who are still ready to bar
the way.*] Let them go on. [*To* DENNIS *as he turns to
go.*] Twenty-four hours. No more.

DENNIS

[*Moves to the left. Pauses. Turns and, with deliber-
ation, calls.*] Riel, you'll hang for this! [*Goes out with*
WEBB *and* THOMAS SCOTT, *to the left.*]

RIEL

[*Struck by the remark.*] Hang for this.

[*His supporters are around him, chattering
excitedly and congratulating him:
"Bravo! Riel! Vive! Monsieur Riel!"*]

MOTHER

Oh Louis. Louis son!

RABBIE

Aye, for a man that's no a Scot you argued it fine.

RIEL

God is with us friends. We will go on in his strength
for without him we are nothing. Join your comrades in
Fort Garry, and do all you do for the honour of
religion and the salvation of your souls.

[*They all move off, up left, chattering:
"Fort Garry." "Riel!" "Thomas Scott."
"Dennis." "Our friends."*]

SCENE 3   *Room in Fort Garry*

A table. A bench or form. At the back a frame over which hangs the Union Jack. This is a room in Fort Garry. Daylight. Lounging are RABBIE, FRANCOIS, XAVIER, *other half-breeds and Indians. All are armed. Their rifles, not necessarily in sight, have been stacked —but their bandoliers are over their shoulders. They have jugs of liquor. Some are smoking cigars.*

RABBIE

Here's tae us, lads. To sittin' snug wi' all the best to eat and drink—pemmican, brandy, baccy—ours wi'out a shot! [*He raises his drink.*]

FRANCOIS

Victoire!

XAVIER

Brava!

> [*They drink the toast. As they are doing so,* O'DONAGHUE *enters briskly from the left, carrying a rolled-up flag of green-and-white cloth.* O'DONAGHUE *wears a tweed knicker bocker suit, and a tie, with belt and pistol.*]

O'DONOGHUE

[*Sharply, sarcastically.*] Victoire! Brava! Without a shot! That's something to be whooping about!

RABBIE

An' what would please you? If some o' us had been killt!

O'DONOGHUE

[*Unfolding the flag.*] You'll have lots of chances to get killed. So save you breath to blow your porridge —in the other place.

RABBIE

Mister O'Donoghue, you pass wi' some folks for an eddicated man [O'DONOGHUE *smiles to himself and grunts.*] so would you favour us wi' your opeenion: Why did McTavish let us march in wi'out a shot?

O'DONOGHUE

Presumably because he wanted us in.

RABBIE

But why, man, why?

O'DONOGHUE

I didn't ask him and he didn't say.

FRANCOIS

[*Very slightly tipsy.*] Monsieur Riel—he prays—he prays. And something happens. They do not close the gates. They do not shoot. We march in.

XAVIER

Like when he prays he makes a miracle.

RABBIE

I hae a strong suspeecion the miracle didna work on Mister McTavish wi'out some sort o' a cash consideration. Suppose, now, suppose, the bosses in London didna gie him his fair whack o' the pig's cheek—the three-hundred-thousand-pounds. What does McTavish do? He tells them to stick it you know where, and just tae spite them he lets us march in wi'out a shot.

FRANCOIS

Ya, ya.

XAVIER

Rabbie is right.

RABBIE

Am I right Mister O'Donoghue?

O'DONOGHUE

I don't know.

RABBIE

Gie a guess man, gie a guess.

O'DONOGHUE

I'm not a guesser.

RABBIE

Och but you're thrawn the day. What's vexin' you sae sore?

FRANCOIS

The Irish—always they are sore.

O'DONOGHUE

[*After unfolding the green-and-white flag, he points to the Union Jack.*] Pull down that rag.

RABBIE

The flag?

O'DONOGHUE

Down with it. Pull it down.

RABBIE

Is he gone daft or what?

FRANCOIS

Monsieur Riel said it will stay, the flag.

O'DONOGHUE

Riel! Riel! [*Pulling the Union Jack down roughly and bundling it.*] There's for Riel and his kowtowing to the [*Kicking the Union Jack under the table.*] English.

RABBIE

Aye, daft. Clean daft.

O'DONOGHUE

[*Preparing to place the green-and-white flag where the Union Jack was.*] Who owns this country anyway? Us? Or the English?

XAVIER

Not the English.

RABBIE

[*Tartly.*] No, nor the Fenian Irish.

O'DONOGHUE

The Fenian Irish would come across the border and help us.

RABBIE

They'd tether us to the tail o' the U.S.A.

O'DONOGHUE

They'd help us to kick the English out and keep out Canada and fly our own flag—fleur-de-lis and shamrock. . . .

[*The green-and-white flag is now in the Union Jack's place. During the last speech,* RIEL *has come in from the left, attended by two armed Métis guards. He carries some papers in his hand, and takes in what has been going on.*]

RIEL

[*Sternly.*] O'Donoghue! I turn my back and you are at this—nonsense.

O'DONOGHUE

[*Belligerently.*] It isn't nonsense.

RIEL

I told you it is not a time to make trouble about flags. Where is the flag that was there? I said it was not to be disturbed. [RIEL *waits for an answer;* O'DONOGHUE *stares defiantly but does not speak.*] I asked, where is it?

O'DONOGHUE

[*Pointing.*] Where it belongs—among the spits and sawdust.

RIEL

[*His voice small and constricted with rage.*] For this, I should have you put in irons. You do not obey. If you will not obey I will make you an example. It is impossible to be in arms and not have discipline. [*Indicating the green-and-white flag.*] Look at this thing! At the moment when everything for the North-West is touch and go you play at schoolboy nonsense about flags.

O'DONOGHUE

It is not schoolboy nonsense.

RIEL

[*Loudly.*] I say it is.

O'DONOGHUE

[*Contemptuously.*] *You* say!

RIEL

[*He regards* O'DONOGHUE *a moment, his eyes blazing. But he controls himself.*] Give me the flag. [*He indicates the Union Jack under the table.*] Pick up the flag and give it to me. [*Pause,* O'DONOGHUE *makes no move.*] You heard me. [O'DONOGHUE *still does not respond.*] O'Donoghue it is an order. I wait. [*Reluctantly* O'DONOGHUE *obeys, picking up the Union Jack and handing it to* RIEL.] Thank you. [*He unfolds the Union Jack and drapes it over and along his extended arm, speaking.*] Do you think it is for nothing I say always we in the North-West are loyal subjects of her Majesty? Do you know why, you Irishman? I am only one little drop Irish. One little drop of Limerick Irish blood. It is not enough to make me lose my senses and to jump and scream and tear down the flag and kick it in the—spits and sawdust. How many men have we? Seven hundred. How many British? Three million. Seven hundred to fight three million. For what? To say [*The Union Jack.*] we do not like this flag. [*The green-and-white flag.*] This one—it is much prettier!

O'DONOGHUE

To talk like that's insulting. You know as well as I do the flag's a symbol. . . .

RIEL

A symbol.

O'DONOGHUE

Of our independence and integrity as a people. I say we should fly it openly and honestly and fight for it to the death and never compromise.

RIEL

[*Keeping his patience with difficulty.*] Mister O'Donoghue—it is very noble to have such sentiments. Fight, for a symbol. Never compromise. And it gets you what? Only to fight. Ah, you Irishmen, up in the sky. But here we are not in Ireland. Here we must stand on the ground and it is sometimes muck below our feet. And you will learn—you have been professor of mathematics and you will learn that in politics also two-and-two sometimes do—except in Ireland—make four.

O'DONOGHUE

It isn't a question of politics but of principle. We're a new people, a nation in the making. We are not British.

RIEL

But we *are* British subjects.

O'DONOGHUE

We shouldn't be.

RIEL

We choose to be.

O'DONOGHUE

If we do it's to our shame.

RIEL

Because we *must* be. Do you know why? So three million British will have the honour of protecting us when we can not protect ourselves.

O'DONOGHUE

Protect us against whom?

RIEL

You ask this! It is too—naive. I think sometimes: to be
a scholar is it also to be a child? To protect us against
whoever would march in to grab and conquer even
if the would-be grabber is Canada—or the U.S.A.
That is why we call England—Mother Country.

O'DONOGHUE

[*Bitterly.*] And go on letting ourselves be strangled
by the blessed old umbilical!

RIEL

[*Hurt, shouting.*] We are not yet strong enough to
stand on our own legs without her.

RABBIE

A sound argument, Mister Riel.

O'DONOGHUE

Contemptible.

RABBIE

[*Raising his drink.*] Here's tae you, man. [*Drinks.*]

RIEL

So, Mister O'Donoghue, we will try first to secure the
substance of independence—our own self-government
here—and after that, perhaps, to think a little about
the—symbol. [*Lightly, turning to the green-and-white
flag.*] I am sorry. It is a pretty flag. Pretty shamrock.
Pretty fleurs-de-lis. Green and white. Very pretty.
But. . . . [*Shakes his head sadly.*] Take it down, please.
[*Waits. No response.*] I ask please, take down that
flag.

O'DONOGHUE

[*Furious.*] It isn't for you to say which flag. It's for
the Council and the Council hasn't decided.

RIEL

[*Also furious.*] It is decided. I am the Council.

O'DONOGHUE

Riel—you dare say that—openly!

RIEL

I order you at once to take it down or I will tear it
down with my own hands. [*In a tense pause* O'DON-
OGHUE *does not move.* RIEL *turns from him and speaks
quietly.*] Some of you, please.

> [*At once* FRANCOIS *and* XAVIER
> *scramble to take it down.*]

O'DONOGHUE

[*Starting forward to prevent them.*] No. No. Don't touch it. If you dare. . . . [*They have pulled it down.*] Oh you—unprincipled, contemptible, cowardly scum! [*He wheels and stalks off, right.*]

RIEL

[*The green-and-white flag.*] Fold it carefully. [FRAN-COIS *and* XAVIER *do so.*] Put this back. [*He gives the Union Jack to the guards who put it up again. A moment later.*] God save the Queen. Say it with me—all—please. [*He says it louder, but not all say it with him.*] God save the Queen. Not all said it. Some are sitting down. [*Anger rising.*] Stand up!

[*Reluctantly, all rise.*]

RABBIE

[*Embarrassed.*] Now, now, Mister Riel, it isna wise to push a good thing sae far it makes us look rideeculous.

RIEL

All say it now.

[*This time it is spoken by all,
in an awkward embarrassed way.*]

ALL

God save the Queen.

RIEL

[*Quietly.*] Thank you. [*To one of the older Métis guards.*] André Nault. [*André stands forward a pace.*] No one will tamper with the flag again, here or on the flagpost in the yard. If anyone tries—you will place a sentry to shoot down anyone who tries, at sight. That is an order, André.

[ANDRE *acknowledges with a nod, and moves towards the flag.* RIEL *turns to go, left. There is general relaxing.* RABBIE *and others sit down again and start to drink.* RIEL *meets the* PRIEST *who enters, left, and bows to him. The* PRIEST *nods acknowledgment and whispers a word to* RIEL *which may be* "drinking." RIEL *turns back. All of this takes only an instant.*]

RIEL

[*To the men.*] I am still here. And the good father. You will please not sit down. [*They stand again.*] There is one other thing. It is what I came at first to say but this flag business. . . . When folks take on themselves to run their own government it is not a soiree—a little pic-nic. It is instead a serious thing to make it work. I asked from everyone sacrifice, discipline. Instead—you have a good time, you laugh, you *drink!*

RABBIE

    If you'll pardon me. . . .

RIEL

    [*Loudly.*]Why not bring in the girls and dance, dance, have music, make whoopee!

RABBIE

    What ails you the day man?

RIEL

    [*At* RABBIE.] You have already drunk too much.

RABBIE

    You're like a body half-demented.

RIEL

    [*Reacting slightly to the last remark.*] Now you will please be quiet. [*To the others.*] I must order—till our position is established—no more drinking.

        [*The* PRIEST *nods approval but others exclaim against it:* "*Monsieur Riel!*" "*No drinking!*" "*But please. . . .*" "*We do not get drunk!*"]

RIEL

    No more liquor will be bought or sold or taken.

RABBIE

    Startin' from when?

RIEL

    From now. I will thank you each to leave your drinks here, and go.

        [*Reluctantly they file past* RIEL *and place their unfinished drinks on the table before him and the* PRIEST. RABBIE *is last. He halts at the table, gazes ruefully into his drink, shakes his head and, deciding he cannot leave it, raises it to drain it. As he does, he speaks.*]

RABBIE

    Naw. It would break my heart. [*He drains it, and planks the pot upside down on the table.*] There you are. Mister Riel. I hae a grreat respect for your abeelity—but man, man, you're in sore need o' a wee touch o' a sense o' humour!

        [*He follows the others out.*]

PRIEST

    [*Smiling in spite of himself.*] So insubordinate.

RIEL

    The Scots, they are *born* insubordinate.

        [*A hullabaloo, off right. Armed* GUARDS *force* THOMAS SCOTT *in before them, manacled. They prod him on.*]

RIEL

This man again.

SCOTT

Aye, you won't get rid of me so easy. I'll fix you yet!
I swore an oath on my holy Bible! I'll fix you yet!

GUARD

We caught him. He had a gun. He said it was for
Monsieur Riel. To shoot. Monsieur Riel.

SCOTT

That's right, that's right.

GUARD

We took the gun.

SCOTT

Gun or no gun I'll fix you yet.

RIEL

Take him away. Keep him in chains this time. This
time he must not escape.

SCOTT

See if I don't. You're a dead man as sure as God.
Aye be Jasus are you, and I'm the boy will send you
tumblin' to hell, you Papish ghet.

[*He is forcibly prodded off left.*]

RIEL

Evil. Evil. He is evil that man. I feel the evil coming
out of him. At me. And at religion. He would destroy
religion. He would destroy—everything here. He goes
about plotting. Shouting against us. Stirring up strife.
Already—he has had his chance. I sent him across the
border, but he comes back. He is sent back, to kill me.
That is what they would have him do. Kill me. Assas-
sinate. . . . Many have urged me to have him marched
before a firing squad. I do not wish this. No! No! I
would not! But—it may have to be.

PRIEST

If he could first be tried.

RIEL

Yes, yes, he will be tried.

PRIEST

And may I suggest by a properly constituted court.

RIEL

By a Court Martial. Adjutant Ambroise Lépine will
summon a Court Martial. Ambroise, with André
Nault, Elzéar Lagimodière, Baptiste Lépine, Joseph
Delorme. . . .

SCENE 4 *Fort Garry Precincts*

RABBIE *and* FRANCOIS, *wearing bandoliers but without rifles, are off duty. They are standing before a posted notice, down left. Throughout this Scene,* FRANCOIS *speaks rapidly and excitedly;* RABBIE, *by contrast, is grave and slow.*

RABBIE

[*Looking up at notice.*] Man-oh-man-oh-man.

FRANCOIS

Six are to shoot him.

RABBIE

Aye, thank God I'm no one o' them.

FRANCOIS

It is near the time. Already I have the jumps.

RABBIE

Three o' the carbines is loaded with blanks. But all the same. . . . [*He shakes his head.*]

FRANCOIS

They had rum. He served the rum himself.

RABBIE

I could do wi' the rum. But naw—not even for the rum. [*He reads from the notice.*] " . . . Court Martial . . . this day tried Thomas Scott, labourer . . . having broken an oath not to take arms against . . . Provisional Government . . . and that also . . . having struck his guards. . . . "

FRANCOIS

Ya, ya, he struck Monsieur Riel. Always he shouts, I will kill Riel, I will kill him. . . . He starts much trouble.

RABBIE

[*Not having taken his eyes from the notice.*] "Verdict of the Court—guilty."

FRANCOIS

Sure he was guilty.

RABBIE

"Sentence of the Court—majority—death."

FRANCOIS

[*Under his breath, crossing himself.*] Death.

RABBIE

" . . . To be executed by a Firing Squad . . . at noon."

[*He turns slowly away from notice.*]

FRANCOIS

Rabbie. We will be late. Come, Rabbie, quick.

RABBIE

Naw.

FRANCOIS

We can see.

RABBIE

Naw, naw.

FRANCOIS

You do not come?

RABBIE

[*Shaking his head.*] Naw, naw, naw. He brought it on himsel', but I hae no great grah tae see him or any ither poor misguided fool blasted into the presence o' his Maker.

FRANCOIS

[*Eager to be off.*] Ya, ya. . . .

RABBIE

I canna help but think it might sae easy 'a' been mysel'.

FRANCOIS
Ya sure. . . .

RABBIE
What!

FRANCOIS
I can not wait.

[*Hurries off, up right.*]

RABBIE
How any decent Christian can relish sich a sight. . . .

[*He shakes his head and goes off, slowly, left.*]

SCENE 5   *Cell in Fort Garry*

The "condemned cell." A spot comes up on corner down right. It picks out SCOTT, *kneeling, manacled. Beside him kneels a Methodist clergyman, the Reverend* MR. YOUNG. SCOTT *is in distress.*

YOUNG

    [*Gravely.*] It's a solemn thing to be passing out of life into eternity. But if you've now truly repented of your sins and taken Jesus into your heart as your Lord and Saviour. . . . [SCOTT *sobs.*] Then, my brother, do not fear or grieve. He won't fail you. He'll be with you, to go hand-in-hand with you through this brief shadow into the eternal glory beyond.

                [*A knocking, as on the cell door.* SCOTT, *fearing the execution call, whimpers and sinks low to the floor.*]

SCOTT

    No. No. Oh no.

VOICE

    The President.

                [*An armed half-breed* GUARD *appears behind* SCOTT. RIEL *follows. The Reverend* MR. YOUNG *stands up and bows.* RIEL *returns the bow.*]

YOUNG

    [*Gently, bending over* SCOTT.] Can you stand up, brother. It's Monsieur Riel, the President. Rise if you can.

                [*He tries to help* SCOTT *up but he remains crouched down in his misery.*]

RIEL

No matter no matter, if he can hear what I come to say.

YOUNG

Thomas Scott, can you hear? Can you?

SCOTT

[*Out of his sobs.*] What, what, oh what?

RIEL

I come myself to ask, even at this last minute, are you prepared to make an end of stirring up revolt, against me and the government here? [*Pause. No answer.*] Thomas Scott, have you heard me?

YOUNG

[*For* scott *to hear.*] You would spare his life?

RIEL

Is he now ready to swear an oath of full loyalty to us . . . to our Government here? [*Pause. Again no answer.*] Are you? [*Pause. No answer. Sharply and angrily.*] Are you? Thomas Scott. Answer!

> [scott *writhes and whimpers like a tortured animal, clenching and unclenching his fists and hammering them on his knees and his head. This takes place through Riel's last questioning. At the final "Thomas Scott. Answer!"* scott *leaps up and shouts hysterically.*]

SCOTT

No! No! That's your answer. Never! Never! No surrender to Papish ghets!

> [*Simultaneously and masking the end of it.*]

YOUNG

Thomas Scott, Thomas Scott, oh my brother I beg you. . . .

> [scott *makes a sudden leap at* RIEL, *swinging his manacled fists.*]

SCOTT

Let me at him. Let me at him. To hell with him. I'll take him with me. I'll see him roastin'. Roastin' in hell!

> [RIEL *has stepped behind the* GUARD *who, helped by the Reverend* MR. YOUNG, *is grappling with* SCOTT.]

SCENE 6 *Room in Fort Garry*

Spot comes up on a small table on which stands a little statue of St. Joseph. Seated at the table are the PRIEST *and* MR. D. A. SMITH, *a deputation.*

SMITH

Not much hope, father.

PRIEST

If Scott himself would help us! But he won't.

> [*They rise at once as* RIEL *enters. He is very agitated, but bows to the deputation.*]

RIEL

I am sorry, father. Sorry Mister Smith. I have seen him. I am very shaken. Nothing will change that man. He is evil. Evil. I tell you [*His voice rises sharply.*] Satan is in him. He *is* Satan. He is Anti-Christ.

SMITH

[*Deprecating.*] Mr. President!

PRIEST

Perhaps having you execute him is Satan's means to wreck your—mission.

RIEL

No. No. [*Gathering himself.*] You have pleaded for him with much eloquence. I thank you. But. . . .

PRIEST

You have shown clemency before. You reprieved Boulton and. . . .

RIEL

Sentence of death is the law's last resort. Clemency always would make it a joke.

SMITH

True, true, but there's the question of expediency. . . .

PRIEST

We think the execution is bound to have very serious consequences in Protestant Ontario. Demands for vengeance. Ottawa would almost certainly be forced to act.

RIEL

Whatever Orange Ontario or Ottawa may do, later, now it is necessary to have acceptance here of our authority. It is my duty as President to compel this, first, before everything. I will not have all we stand for put in jeopardy by endless plotting against us. This execution, now, in a few minutes, of this devil, this, this. . . . [*Controlling himself with difficulty.*] The prisoner, Scott, may bring our trouble-makers to their senses. He has been found guilty by Court Martial. The majority was for death. And he must die. If he did not, something of much importance—more than his life—might perish—our Government and all we hope from it. [*Relaxing his more or less formal tone, to one gentle and most polite.*] So, for the Christian charity that brought you here, my humble thanks. That is all.

> [*He bows in dismissal. The* PRIEST
> *and* SMITH *bow in return.*]

SMITH

Thank you Mr. President.

PRIEST

There is no more we can say or do?

RIEL

Only what I myself beg leave to do—to pray, for his soul.

> [*They go out, left. As they leave, Riel's*
> MOTHER *enters quickly, passing them and bowing*
> *to the* PRIEST. *She is very agitated.*]

MOTHER

Pardon. Louis. It is the time. They have marched him out. It is noon. In a moment you will hear it strike. I thought if you would let me . . . to be with you, when. . . .

RIEL

No, please. No one with me.

MOTHER

But me? Not me, Louis?

RIEL

No one.

Louis. . . .

> [*Because of something in his manner, she turns
> reluctantly away and goes, left. As she leaves
> a large clock off stage begins to strike the four
> quarters of the hour, and goes on to strike
> twelve.* RIEL, *alone now, sits heavily at the
> little table and clutches the statue of St. Joseph
> in his hands. His head drops to the crook of his arm
> on the table. He stands up, clutching the statue,
> listens with eyes closed and lips moving as the
> clock goes on striking. He is very agitated.
> After the fifth stroke, he speaks.*]

RIEL

Lord have mercy on us.

> [*Sixth stroke*]

Christ hear us.

> [*Seventh stroke*]

Christ graciously hear us.

> [*Eighth stroke*]

God the Father in Heaven have mercy on us.

> [*Ninth stroke*]

God the Son, Redeemer of the world, have mercy on
us.

> [*Tenth stroke*]

God the Holy Ghost have mercy on us.

> [*Eleventh stroke*]

Holy Trinity One God have mercy on us.

> [*Twelfth stroke*]

Holy Mary pray for us.

> [RIEL *stands rigid, waiting.*]

VOICE OF COMMAND

> [*Off, up right.*]

Ready!
Present!
Fire!

> [*The volley of the Firing Squad
> shatters the silence.*]

RIEL

[*Overcome.*] Me too. My life too. My life too it is
taken. This will be. This will be. Oh there is blood
and blood.

SCENE 7 *An Open Place in Ontario*

*A mob spectacle which may be included or not accord-
ing to the resources of the production. It may be
staged as a night spectacle, with torches and the glow
of bonfires. Orange drums are heard somewhere in the
background. The clamour of an approaching mob is
heard. The mob swarms on the stage, a yelling, gesticulating, fanatical mass of people, farmers, artisans,
in working clothes. They are armed with sticks and
some have the brass-spiked poles used by sidesmen at
Orange processions. They carry flags and boards
hoisted on poles with roughly painted legends: "Hang
Riel," "Vengeance for Thomas Scott," "March on Red
River." Carried high is an effigy hanging from a scaffold and labelled "Riel." The key words that keep
recurring in the frenzied shouting are: Riel, Murder,
Scott, Orangeman, Revenge. They occur in such
phrases as: "Hang Riel!" "Murder in Red River!"
"Orangeman Thomas Scott—murdered!" "Who murdered Thomas Scott?" "Riel!" "Revenge for Thomas
Scott!" As the mob moves across the stage, the lights
rapidly dim and the noise dwindles rapidly to silence
and black out.*

SCENE 8 *Fort Garry Precincts*

Light comes up on an outdoor scene. Bright morning.
RABBIE *stands reading some sensational headlines from
a newspaper.* FRANCOIS *and* XAVIER *come along and
join him, looking glum.*

RABBIE
[*Reading aloud.*] "Hang Riel!" "Revenge for Thomas
Scott!" "Orangeman murdered!" "Ontario up in arms!"

FRANCOIS
Trouble for Louis! Much trouble!

XAVIER
Like you say, "the fat it is in the fire."

RABBIE
Aye, the fat's in the fire now all right! [*Again reading
aloud.*] "All Ontario ablaze!" [*Recognizing a jingle in
the paper.*] Hi! Look what's here! "We'll hang him up
the river, with your yah, yah, yah!" I mind them yelling that one—back in the old country when the blood
was up. [*He sings it.*]

We'll hang him up the river/with your yah, yah, yah!
We'll hang him up the river/with your yah, yah, yah!
We'll hang him up the river
And he'll roast in hell for ever/with your yah! yah!
Yah, Yah, Yah!

[*The* PRIEST *and* SMITH *have come
along and halted.*]

SMITH

He'll roast in hell for ever?

RABBIE

Riel. If Ontario has its way.

PRIEST

It's true. Ontario's gone mad. Toronto. Every town big or little. Wherever Orangemen meet—hang Riel! Revenge for Thomas Scott.

SMITH

Nasty situation.

PRIEST

Nasty for Ottawa.

SMITH

Getting out of hand. . . .

PRIEST

Very dangerous.

SMITH

But, I trust John A.

PRIEST

[*Not understanding it.*] John-nie?

SMITH

Macdonald. Sir John A. Prime Minister.

PRIEST

Of course of course.

SMITH

He'll know how to cope with it.

PRIEST

He'll need all his guile.

SMITH

Scots canniness.

PRIEST

Same thing. Commodity he's well endowed with.

SMITH

Aye. And he has good advice. The best. Cartier. Bishop Taché.

PRIEST

The Bishop? In Ottawa? He *was* in Rome. The Ecumenical. . . .

SMITH

> Macdonald called him back post-haste.

PRIEST

> Then—there may be some hope. First ray of hope!

SMITH

> He knows his flock out here.

PRIEST

> To him at least, they aren't just—savages.

RABBIE

> Macdonald and the Bishop! Man-oh-man-oh-man! I'd gie a siller poun' to hae one keek at *that* set-to!

SCENE 9 *Prime Minister's Room, Ottawa*

Light comes up on the Prime Minister's room at Ottawa. In conference are MACDONALD, CARTIER, TACHE *and* WOLSELEY. *Somewhere outside a demonstrating mob is roughly singing "We'll hang him up the river."* MACDONALD *and the others listen for a few moments. The mob's singing dwindles during the speeches that follow.*

MACDONALD
Barbarians! Barbarians! Rank barbarians!

CARTIER
[*Slyly.*] *Orange* barbarians.

MACDONALD
Orange barbarians.

TACHE
Alas, Sir John, that comment cannot be overheard by your Ontario constituencies.

MACDONALD
Your Grace is privileged. Fortunately for you the Church doesn't depend on the whims of an electorate.

WOLSELEY
Ditto the Army.

MACDONALD
However, gentlemen, to turn from these pleasantries to the business before us, let us first get a clear view of the facts. The North-West Territories are still outside Confederation. We need them in. Riel is master there.

[*The mob's singing outside has now died out.*]

WOLSELEY

A madman, Riel! Utterly mad!

TACHE

Colonel Wolseley, please!

WOLSELEY

Stark, staring mad!

MACDONALD

Mad he may be, though I've a notion he's merely mad
—Nor'-Nor'-West!

[TACHE *and* CARTIER *deprecate the pun.*]

MACDONALD

In any case he runs rings round the pompous blun-
derers who've acted for us out there: McDougall and
Stoughton Dennis.

TACHE

They couldn't have done more to compromise your
Government with Riel and my flock. They've opened
an abyss. . . .

MACDONALD

Aye, it's a mistake, to send out overwashed would-be
Englishmen utterly ignorant of the country and just as
full of crochets as all Englishmen are. . . .

WOLSELEY

I take strong exception to that remark!

MACDONALD

I except the army. . . .

WOLSELEY

Crochets! *Crochets!*

MACDONALD

Especially the Officers Corps where crochets, of course,
are unknown. However . . . [*He helps himself to
snuff.*] by the grace of God and the gumption of this
extraordinary person Riel, the Provisional Government
headed by him is willing to enter Confederation with
us and become a province of Canada—on Riel's terms,
of course. [*Sneezes.*] He showed his astuteness in re-
fusing to let our blockhead representative McDougall
even cross the border till the terms are signed.

WOLSELEY

Surely he had no right to act in such a dastardly high-
handed way!

CARTIER

Perhaps he had.

MACDONALD

There's no doubt of it.

TACHE

You admit this, Sir John?

MACDONALD

[*Pauses. He glances at him, pointedly.*] I do—to you.

TACHE

[*Acknowledging it.*] Of course. I understand.

WOLSELEY

I don't.

MACDONALD

My view is that on the Hudson's Bay Company's withdrawal no legal government existed, leaving a state of anarchy. In such cases the inhabitants may by the law of nations form a government, *ex necessitate*, for the protection of life and property. And such a government has certain sovereign rights by the *jus gentium*. This is laid down by Blackstone. A most important principle. And it is precisely what this—allegedly mad but actually very astute—creature Riel has had the gumption to grasp and act upon.

CARTIER

It makes entirely legal the status of himself and his Provisional Government?

TACHE

And also whatever actions they may have thought necessary to preserve their authority?

WOLSELEY

[*Sarcastically.*] Including the murder of Thomas Scott I daresay!

TACHE

The *execution.* . . .

WOLSELEY

Murder. Murder I said and murder I mean. In my opinion. . . .

MACDONALD

If you'll bear with me Colonel it isn't a matter for military opinion. And meanwhile what we're considering is whether we've any right to enter the territory of Riel's government without their consent. At present I think we have none whatever—no more than we have to enter the U.S.A. at Buffalo or any other port without the U.S.A.'s consent. Riel knows this—and stands us off—till we negotiate specific terms, and sign. He has set out these terms very ably in a Bill of Rights.

This Bill—with the anxious approval and blessing of Her Majesty's Imperial Government in London— Fenian and other annexationist forces in the U.S.A. not lost sight of—we shall make the basis of an Act incorporating the North-West with Canada. . . .

CARTIER

Here, here.

MACDONALD

A new Province in Confederation. And I think we may say that Riel has fathered this new Province. He has even proposed to name it—Manitoba.

WOLSELEY

Name of some Red Indian god or bogeyman or something?

MACDONALD

I understand the word is Indian for "the god who speaks."

WOLSELEY

Meaning Riel himself!

MACDONALD

Manitoba—the god who speaks: from Manitou—the Great Spirit. My two Indian words!

TACHE

Congratulations, Prime Minister, on acquiring the native language of your country—to that extent!

MACDONALD

Touché [*Smiles and adds.*] Taché. [*For Wolseley's benefit.*] Our good friend Taché has interrupted his visit to Rome to help with his wild people out there.

TACHE

With my—*people.*

MACDONALD

With his people. He takes with him assurances of a general amnesty.

WOLSELEY

Is it supposed to cover the cold-blooded murder of Thomas Scott?

MACDONALD

It is intended to assuage passion by all means—to help the setting-up of the new Province.

WOLSELEY

My orders are to proceed with my forces to Fort Garry. Once there I shall certainly make short work of —assuaging passion.

MACDONALD

We're glad to have given Colonel Wolseley the chance of glory, and the risk of the scalping knife. We shall watch him march off with pride. . . .

WOLSELEY

[*Stiffly.*] Thank you.

MACDONALD

And perhaps a little amusement. . . .

WOLSELEY

Amusement!

MACDONALD

An engaging, an almost symbolic, British figure, sallying forth clasping an olive branch in one hand and a pistol in the other.

WOLSELEY

I resent this tone. I'm a soldier. Unlike politicians we soldiers prefer plain speech and plain dealing. I ask, is the scoundrel who murdered Thomas Scott to escape punishment?

MACDONALD

Colonel Wolseley, I know that, because of this most unfortunate affair of Scott, recruiting for your volunteers is brisk in Ontario. But I remind you that your expedition to Fort Garry was organized long before we had news of Scott. Its purpose hasn't changed. You're going out there not to punish Riel or anyone else but. . . .

WOLSELEY

I am going out there to see that the waves of immigrants you mean to send are not molested.

MACDONALD

You are going out there simply to keep order—till the new Governor arrives and takes over from Riel.

WOLSELEY

I will keep order—but certainly not under this criminal blackguard Riel.

MACDONALD

Riel will formally hand over to Governor Archibald. . . . [*Pauses. With careful point.*] I am making this very clear. . . .

WOLSELEY

For the benefit of an obtuse soldier.

MACDONALD

For the benefit of all whom it may concern, now and hereafter: Till Governor Archibald has taken over we recognize Riel as head of the government out there. . . .

WOLSELEY

When I arrive. . . .

MACDONALD

I've no doubt Riel will receive you with all ceremony and the height of courtesy—for which, I understand, he is remarkable . . . [*With a twinkle at Cartier and Taché.*] even among his French compatriots.

TACHE *and* CARTIER

[*Together, bowing and smiling.*] Merci! Merci!

MACDONALD

H'm. Do you think *that* comment has been overheard by the—Quebec constituencies?

CARTIER

I shall certainly see that it echoes around Quebec.

MACDONALD

I have often been grateful for Quebec's remarkable acoustic properties!

WOLSELEY

[*A grunted aside.*] Politicians! Same everywhere!

[MACDONALD *rises, the others follow.*]

MACDONALD

And now with your permission, gentlemen, I'll resume my game of Patience.

[*They exchange bows.* MACDONALD *turns to go, left.* WOLSELEY *marches off right.*]

WOLSELEY

[*As before.*] Politicians! Pah!

MACDONALD

[*Turning back.*] It might be as well, Monseigneur Taché, if you could reach Fort Garry *before* the Colonel and his—volunteers.

CARTIER

I share Sir John's misgivings. What with Wolseley's unhelpful attitude and this ugly clamour to hang Riel —we have a very explosive situation indeed.

TACHE

I pray to God nothing may go amiss.

MACDONALD *and* CARTIER

Amen.

SCENE 10 *Fort Garry Precincts*

RABBIE, *sauntering along, is met by* O'DONOGHUE, *who is hurrying in the opposite direction.* RABBIE *halts him. Neither has rifle nor bandolier. Outdoors.*

RABBIE

You're an eddicated man, Mister O'Donoghue.

O'DONOGHUE

Eddicated?

RABBIE

Aye, eddicated.

O'DONOGHUE

If you call me that again I'll smother you with your own sporran!

RABBIE

Man, man, you're no ashamed o' your superior eddication are you!

O'DONOGHUE

What do you want my opeenion on this time?

RABBIE

What else but the big news.

O'DONOGHUE

[*Rapidly.*] If you mean do I think Wolseley and his Orange volunteers are coming here with anything in mind but the old, old British game of perfidy—the answer is I don't.

[*He starts on his way again.*]

RABBIE

[*Detaining him.*] Now what kind o' a connotation hae you in mind for the word perfidy?

O'DONOGHUE

Fair promises—then the yoke on the neck and the whip-lash on the back. The same old [*Mimics Rabbie.*] connotation. Good-day to you.

[*Again trying to be off.*]

RABBIE

[*Again detaining him.*] Bide a bit, Mister O'Donoghue.

O'DONOGHUE

What now?

RABBIE

You hae vouchsafed only a sort o' a general answer; but, in parteecular, now. . . .

O'DONOGHUE

If in particular you mean do I think Wolseley and his Orange riff-raff have the least intention of forgetting about Thomas Scott and sitting down instead to smoke the pipe of peace with Ex-Monsieur-le-Président Louis Riel—again the answer is—I don't.

RABBIE

In your considered opeenion, then. . . .

O'DONOGHUE

[*Loudly.*] Riel's a fool!

[*This time he briskly moves along and goes off.*]

RABBIE

[*Gazing after him.*] Man-oh-man-oh-man!

[*He turns and resumes his meditative stroll in the opposite direction.*]

SCENE 11 *Room in Fort Garry*

*As the light comes up, there is applause from a group
of people, Riel's supporters: members of the Council,
volunteers—but neither* O'DONOGHUE *nor* FRANCOIS *is
among them. They are gathered in a room at Fort
Garry, and they stand listening to* RIEL, *who now wears
a formal black frock coat, with a "Gladstone" wide-
wing collar. He carries a silk tall-hat in his hands. But
he is wearing moccasins.* TACHE *hovers in the background, listening with anxious attention. Something is
affecting* RIEL. *In his voice there is evidence of feeling
controlled only with difficulty. This becomes increas-
ingly noticeable as he proceeds.*

RIEL

So, we have prepared a reception. A great reception.
To celebrate the setting-up of this new Province . . .
in Confederation. And to honour the arrival, here, of
the first [*He hesitates.*] Governor . . . with Colonel
Wolseley and his troops. We shall fire a salute of can-
non, and provide an escort of as many horsemen as we
can muster. I have sent forward my . . . personal . . .
respects . . . to . . . Governor Archibald. [*This is
received with dissenting cries:* "No!" "No!" "We want
you!" "Riel for Governor!" "Governor Riel!" RIEL *cuts
in.*] No, no, no. I thank you but it is not my wish.
[*With sudden sharp emphasis.*] It is not my wish to
be Governor! [*Pause. He recovers himself. Then, continues quietly.*] I beg you, please. You know I have
said always I wish to have power only till I can hand
it on. For the best interests of religion and of you my
own people here. Now, it is the time to . . . hand on . . .
[*He stops abruptly. Sways. Steadies himself.*] That is
all. I thank you. Please go now.

[*They are puzzled and murmur in concern, but they bow and file out. When they have gone,* RIEL *slumps.* TACHE *comes to him, very concerned.*]

TACHE

Monsieur! Monsieur Riel! What is it?

RIEL

Nothing, nothing, I am nothing.

TACHE

But at this moment—of your victory!

RIEL

Victory. [*With sudden vehemence.*] He is a fine man Archibald!

[*This* non sequitur *and the violence of it strikes* TACHE, *but he is unsure of the import.*]

TACHE

Yes. Yes.

RIEL

[*Fiercely.*] A fine man!

TACHE

I pray he may prove so.

[RIEL *crushes his silk hat and tosses it aside. He is very agitated.* TACHE *is horrified.* RIEL *drops to his knees.*]

RIEL

Will you bless me, will you bless me?

TACHE

Yes, my son, yes.

RIEL

I will say a prayer, may I say a prayer?

TACHE

What prayer?

RIEL

[*Crying out.*] Oh my Father, help me! Help me—to—accept—endure—this.

TACHE

[*Gently.*] You may say that prayer.

RIEL

If this be thy will. According to the views of thy Providence—which are beautiful and without measure.

[*There is a loud scuffling and hullabaloo.*
O'DONOGHUE *is trying to break in and
an armed guard is trying to prevent him.*]

VOICE OF GUARD

You can not. You can not go in. We have orders.

VOICE OF O'DONOGHUE

[*Simultaneously.*] I must! I must go in! Out of my
way! It's life or death!

[O'DONOGHUE *forces his way in, left, standing off
the* GUARD. *The* GUARD *retires and* O'DONOGHUE
comes excitedly forward. RIEL *rises and
with* TACHE *he turns on* O'DONOGHUE *with shock
and resentment.*]

RIEL

O'Donoghue!

TACHE

Mr. O'Donoghue!

RIEL

How dare you. . . .

TACHE

What is the meaning. . . .

O'DONOGHUE

Perfidy. In one word—perfidy.

RIEL *and* TACHE

Perfidy?

O'DONOGHUE

The old, old story. I warned you. Wolseley! The British
soldiers! The Orangemen volunteers! They're here. A
few hours march. We could have stopped them. Cut
them in pieces. But it's too late. . . . There are a dozen
strategic points where we could have [*He shouts.*]
decimated them! And the Fenians would have helped.

RIEL

They are against the Church the Fenians.

O'DONOGHUE

Nonsense, nonsense, that old idiotic lie.

TACHE

It's neither nonsense nor a lie—the Fenians are a secret
society and as such banned by the Church.

O'DONOGHUE

All right, all right, all right, welcome the Orangemen. Welcome Wolseley. He'll spring his steel trap on you while you welcome him.

TACHE

Mr. O'Donoghue, you are grievously mistaken. Colonel Wolseley has precise instructions, from London and Ottawa.

O'DONOGHUE

He's on his own, thousands of miles from London and Ottawa. . . .

TACHE

He must obey instructions.

O'DONOGHUE

He'll do what he wants to do out here and square it after with—instructions.

TACHE

We will not argue. You will please not go further.

O'DONOGHUE

I must.

TACHE

In that case I am not prepared to listen. [*He turns pointedly away.*] Monsieur Riel, you have the assurances of the ministers and my personal assurance. Count on my presence and support when the Colonel and Governor Archibald arrive.

RIEL

Thank you, Monseigneur.

[*He bows as* TACHE *goes out, left.*]

O'DONOGHUE

Oh, Riel, you *are* a fool! [RIEL *merely turns away.*] Listen. . . .

RIEL

[*Listlessly.*] I have the Proclamation of Wolseley, signed by himself. [*He produces it and prepares to read.*]

O'DONOGHUE

[*Regarding it with impatient scepticism.*] Proclamation! That he's coming here to grab the land, and fight to keep it for Macdonald's immigrants.

RIEL

[*Reading.*] "My mission is one of peace. . . ."

O'DONOGHUE

Of course, of course, the old, old trick.

RIEL

"The forces I have the honour of commanding will enter your Province representing no party, either in religion or politics. . . ."

O'DONOGHUE

No party! His Orangemen no party, it makes me laugh!

RIEL

"We will afford equal protection to the lives and property of all races and creeds. . . ."

O'DONOGHUE

Equal protection no protection, nothing equal to nothing. The old perfidious game. Soothe them with syrup. Get their confidence. Then—pounce.

RIEL

[*Without conviction.*] I will not believe this.

[*The scene begins to darken.*]

O'DONOGHUE

Riel you *do* believe it. That's what's eating your heart. [RIEL *turns away and sits on the chair.*] Why do you *want* this, to be trapped! [*Sure he has a clue.*] Look at him! Look! The noble patriot, betrayed! The tragic man! [*Their eyes meet.* RIEL *says nothing.* O'DONOGHUE *closes in.*] The Orangemen came a thousand miles to have your blood—they'll have your blood and march back with your battered head mounted for trophy on an Orange drum. [*Slight pause. Finally, exasperated past bearing, he shouts.*] Why do you sit there in a daze—waiting for them to strike! Could Wolseley stop his Orangemen even if he wanted to? [*Himself almost hysterical.*] Riel! [*No response. Giving it up.*] All right, you want it and you won't have long to wait.

[*The* GUARD *has come in from the left.*]

GUARD

Monsieur Riel. François is here.

[RIEL *rises.*]

RIEL

Bring him. [*The* GUARD *goes to bring François. To* O'DONOGHUE.] I sent François to find out.

O'DONOGHUE

To spy.

RIEL

Now I will talk to him—please, alone.

When Wolseley comes count on my presence too, in
support—but with my gun.

[O'DONOGHUE *goes quickly out, right, as* FRANCOIS
enters, left. FRANCOIS *is a little out of breath,
dishevelled, wet and mud-bespattered.
He is very agitated.*]

RIEL

You travelled fast.

FRANCOIS

The news. It could not wait.

RIEL

Tell me.

FRANCOIS

The Colonel Wolseley, already he takes prisoners.

RIEL

Prisoners?

FRANCOIS

The folks who went there from Fort Garry. To see
him come. To shout Brava.

RIEL

He seized them? [FRANCOIS *nods in assent.*] He seized
these unarmed folk?

FRANCOIS

Ya. Ya.

[*A slight pause.* RIEL *steadies himself.*]

RIEL

What more, François?

FRANCOIS

I saw many things. I did not like what I saw. The
soldiers. The *volunteers.* They shout. They shake the
fist. They say, "There will be some hangings in Fort
Garry! Some French will hang."

RIEL

You heard this?

FRANCOIS

And always they talk of Scott. Revenge for Scott. They
say. . . . [*He hesitates.*] Pardon, Monsieur Riel. I tell
only what they say. . . .

RIEL

What?

FRANCOIS

"Monsieur Riel he will be first to hang, tomorrow."

RIEL

François, I was prepared to welcome them.

FRANCOIS

They sing a song, "We'll hang him up the river. . . ."

RIEL

Please, it is enough. François I have one question. The answer to it will tell, everything. [*Carefully.*] The Governor—Archibald. Is he in camp with Wolseley? Does he come here with Wolseley?

FRANCOIS

This I know. He is not with them. He does not come for many days.

RIEL

[*A slight pause. Then quietly, as to himself.*] Then it is—perfidy. [*Pause. He reflects. Then suddenly he seizes the Proclamation, tears it in two and flings it on the floor. He shouts.*] Proclamation! Perfidy! [*He makes a gesture of contempt, then turns briskly to* FRANCOIS.] Where do they camp tonight?

FRANCOIS

At Grenouillière.

RIEL

I will go there.

FRANCOIS

Monsieur Riel!

RIEL

Now. At once. I will make sure.

FRANCOIS

If they take you!

RIEL

[*With pistol.*] They will not take me.

FRANCOIS

It pours rain. It pours now, everywhere. Much rain! Everywhere it will be dark, dark.

[*The scene is now almost dark.*]

RIEL

Dark, dark everywhere! Come, François.

[*They go, quickly.*]

SCENE 12   *Room in Fort Garry*

Room, as before, in Fort Garry. It is daylight, the next morning. The Union Jack is draped at the back. The torn halves of the Proclamation are still on the floor. TACHE *and* O'DONOGHUE. O'DONOGHUE *is armed, and dishevelled.* TACHE *paces to and fro.*

TACHE

Poor man, poor man.

O'DONOGHUE

The rain was from the north. Cold rain. It poured, all night. Downpour. Deluge. The roar of it, pounding down! You could hardly hear your neighbour shouting in your ear. No, nor see him either, it was so dark. Riel says he could hardly see Baptiste Nault nor Pierre Champagne riding beside him, so close, their knees were rubbing his.

TACHE

So they were with him?

O'DONOGHUE

And Colonel Gay and St. Luc, and François. For once Louis was armed like the rest, from head to foot.

TACHE

Thank God they had no chance to use their arms.

O'DONOGHUE

A great relief to Louis. No love for guns.

TACHE

What time did they get back?

O'DONOGHUE

One of the morning. I was back when they came in.
Drowned. Like myself. Shivering. Cluttered with mud.
Riel threw off his seeping overcoat and shoes, and
tumbled on the bed in a couple of heavy blankets.

TACHE

He got *some* sleep?

O'DONOGHUE

Not much.　About an hour.　He was up.　Sorting his
papers out.　Getting ready to leave.

TACHE

He must be worn out.

O'DONOGHUE

But the way it takes him, he's ready to drop, one minute. Next, he's rushing about, giving orders. Cool and
calm one minute, then walking up and down wringing
his hands like someone half-demented. His eyes are red
and swollen. Last night exhausted him.

TACHE

He took a fearful risk to go near the camp. How near
did he go?

O'DONOGHUE

Close enough. He saw the glow of the fires and went
on, close. Right up to the sentries and outposts.

TACHE

Fearful risk.

O'DONOGHUE

The horses nearly gave them away. *They* knew something was up. Started to whinney and snort. But Louis
had seen all he needed to see. He turned back.

TACHE

Mercifully.

O'DONOGHUE

Just in time. Wolseley's pack was on his heels. Forced
march. Through the mud. Knee-deep in mud. They've
closed in now, all round the Fort. Some of the Orangemen—wearing their regalia!

TACHE

The British, I trust, will be a steadying influence.

O'DONOGHUE

They won't. They can't. The Orangemen in the pack
are panting to get at Riel, slavering for the kill.

TACHE

If only he had left in time! He ordered everyone else to leave.

O'DONOGHUE

He could still leave. They've left us the River Gate. I suppose hoping we'll run for it so they can shoot us down. Why have you stayed, Monseigneur?

TACHE

To receive Wolseley.

O'DONOGHUE

So have I—to receive him—with lead. Ambroise Lépine's still here. Myself. And others. Even the few of us should man the guns and fight.

TACHE

I will fight. Oh I will fight. [o'donoghue *looks surprised and pleased.*] But where my fight may be of use. [*Unobserved,* RIEL *comes in, left. His appearance agrees with* o'donoghue's *description of him.*] I shall go at once, the weary trail again to Ottawa. I will plead. . . .

RIEL

Not for me, Monseigneur. Please no pleading for me.

TACHE

You must allow me. I will communicate at once with London. [*Touched by his dejected appearance.*] Ah, Monsieur, Monsieur. . . . Her Majesty will be grieved, she will. . . .

RIEL

I am not now a—loyal subject of Her Majesty.

O'DONOGHUE

Riel! At last! [*Glances at the flag, alight with his intention.*] Now I can tear it down.

[*He rushes to Union Jack, seizes it and, as before, rips it down and kicks it below the table. Neither* TACHE *nor* RIEL *betray interest in this violent action, nor in what* o'donoghue *presently says and does.*]

TACHE

[*To* RIEL.] I beg you—if you can be patient in this evil —all will come right.

[RIEL *begins laughing, hysterical laughter.*]

TACHE

Riel!

O'DONOGHUE

My compliments to Colonel Wolseley. . . .

RIEL

      Pardon, Monseigneur, pardon, if I laugh now. . . .

O'DONOGHUE

      Say I'll be back with friends to greet him, soon. Fenians!

RIEL

      What do I do now but laugh. . . .

O'DONOGHUE

      Fenians will fight! Fenians at least will fight!

> [*He leaves indignantly, right, neither* RIEL *nor* TACHE *paying attention.*]

RIEL

      [*Thrusting the phrases out in an ascending pitch between starts of laughing.*] I know by the Grace of God. . . . I am the founder of Manitoba. . . . But now, already at its birth. . . . Is it not funny, Monseigneur. . . . I am to fly. . . . I am to. . . . Hide! Monsieur le Président to hide. : . . An outlaw. . . . Riel. . . . In exile. . . .[*Laughter now changes to sobs.*] Oh Monseigneur, Monseigneur, this is my victory!

TACHE

      [*Distressed by it.*] Yes, yes, Monsieur Riel it is still your victory.

RIEL

      My great victory!

TACHE

      Yes. Whatever it may seem for the moment my son. Time will prove it. But now. Come, come, brace yourself. Now you must brace yourself to do what is best to do—the most difficult of all—to leave when victory is won—to turn your back on victory and wait—in prayer and patience saving yourself, for whatever work God yet may call on you to do.

> [*Off, at first at some distance, but drawing close as this incident proceeds, a rabble of soldiery is beginning to run amock. A* GUARD, *armed, comes in, left.*]

GUARD

      Monseigneur! Monsieur Riel! They are in the Fort! Crossing the yard.

> [*Retires again, left.*]

TACHE

      My son, go, go quickly, wait for God's time.

RIEL

      God's time!

> [GUARD *again, very agitated.*]

GUARD

   The Colonel Wolseley! He comes here!

TACHE

   [*Urging Riel.*] Go! Go, my son. It is God's will.

RIEL

   I will come back. I will come back!

       [RIEL *goes off, right, in a distracted manner.*]

TACHE

   [*To the* GUARD.] Go with him.

               [*The* GUARD *hurries after* RIEL.
         TACHE *turns to receive Wolseley. At left,*
         a red-coat SERGEANT *enters with his carbine*
               at the ready. He looks around sharply.]

SERGEANT

   Oh! Excuse me your Reverence. 'Oos 'ere as well as
   you?

TACHE

   No one.

SERGEANT

   [*Advancing into the room, but alert.*] Thank you, your
   Reverence.   Excuse me.

           [*He makes a rapid examination.*]

TACHE

   [*Sternly.*] I said there is no one here.

SERGEANT

   We likes to make sure—but no offense, your Reverence,
   no offense. [*Having satisfied himself, he returns to the
   left, takes his stance and calls through, "O.K., sir." He
   stands at attention as* WOLSELEY *comes in.*]

WOLSELEY

   [*At once seeing* TACHE *and advancing to greet him.*]
   Ah, Your Grace, we meet again!

TACHE

   It is not a pleasure.

WOLSELEY

   [*Momentarily taken aback.*] What! Oh!

TACHE

   You had express instructions that on arrival here. . . .

WOLSELEY

   My instructions were *my* instructions. Your Grace will
   permit me to interpret them according to my own—no
   doubt inferior—judgment. [*Being infuriating.*] It seems
   I'm to be spared the painful duty of dealing with
   this [*Implying "scoundrel."*] . . . with Riel.

[*Outside the rabble are singing:
"We'll hang him up the river."*]

TACHE

I will make it my business to see that not only the
Prime Minister and the Governor General of Canada,
but Her Majesty—and her Majesty's minister in Whitehall the Earl of Granville—are fully informed of this,
this—I scarcely know how to characterize it—this
creditable exploit!

[TACHE *turns and walks indignantly out, right.*]

WOLSELEY

Look here, Bishop. . . . [*But* TACHE *goes on.*] Oh confound these interfering clergy. Can't be content with
managing men's souls. [*He sees the Union Jack under
the table.*] Hullo! [*Picks it up.*] Part of our welcome
from Riel no doubt. [*He listens to the rough singing,
now of: "We'll hang him up the river."*] They'll hang
him up the river. H'm! [*To the* SERGEANT, *referring to
the singing and the tipsy hullabaloo now mounting to
an ugly climax.*] Bless me, isn't it a rumpus!

SERGEANT

Yessir! Men runnin' a bit wild, sir. Lootin' the liquor,
sir.

WOLSELEY

What liquor?

SERGEANT

'Ee 'ad it all locked up, sir. Strict t't' 'ee was.

WOLSELEY

Yes, yes, mad, quite mad.

SERGEANT

Yessir. Our men don't 'old with no t't' nonsense sir, not
after marchin' a thousand miles with their tongues
'angin' out as you might say, sir.

WOLSELEY

Looting the liquor!

[*He listens.*]

SERGEANT

Yes, sir. The lucky ones as is off duty, sir. Won't be
much left by mornin', sir.

WOLSELEY

Sergeant, are you conveying a subtle hint?

SERGEANT

'Int, sir! Oh no, sir!

WOLSELEY

Because it would be highly irregular and unsoldierly.

SERGEANT

Yessir.

WOLSELEY

But your tongue *is* hanging out, as you might say?

SERGEANT

Yessir.

WOLSELEY

What!

SERGEANT

Oh no, sir, no sir.

WOLSELEY

Which is it?

SERGEANT

Well sir, if you was to say, "Sergeant, 'ow abat joinin'
your comrades-in-arms. . . ."

WOLSELEY

Sergeant, how about joining your comrades-in-arms?

SERGEANT

At the double, sir.

WOLSELEY

At the double, Sergeant.

SERGEANT

Yessir. Thank you, sir. Won't see my 'eels for stour,
sir!

[He salutes and hurries out, left.]

WOLSELEY

[Amused by the SERGEANT, *he smiles. He listens a
moment to the uproar, then sees and picks up the torn
Proclamation. He snorts.]* My proclamation! Very
well, very well, if that's how you'd have it! [*He
crushes it and, as he kicks it from him, speaks contemptuously.*] Riel! [*Outside, drunken singing and
uproar. If the resources of a particular production
warrant it, "Hang him up the river" could now be
effectively accompanied by kettle drums, big drum
and flute. For the first time shots are heard, desultory
shooting. With the shots, loud cries of outrage and
protest, pierced by a woman's prolonged scream, are
heard.*]

RIEL: PART TWO

SCENE 1 *Porch of Riel's House, Montana*

RIEL *and* MARGUERITE. *They sit on rickety chairs. Out-doors. Riel is fifteen years older. His clothes are shab-bier. A cross hangs on his breast. He wears a toque. He is sitting a little apart from* MARGUERITE, *his mind wholly concerned with two letters which he holds in his hands. He considers their contents, giving an occa-sional glance at the letters.* MARGUERITE, *his wife, is a half-breed Indian in her early twenties. She is sewing some child's garment. She keeps glancing at Riel, in growing irritation, and is several times about to speak. Finally she does.*

MARGUERITE

Louis. [RIEL *glances at her, not speaking.*] What is it, Louis?

RIEL

What is what?

MARGUERITE

A long time you do not speak. You do not look. You sit there. Sometimes you read the letters. Then you close your eyes. You—think. Your thoughts are not here. It is the same every day.

RIEL

Every day, I think it is a long time I am an exile.

> [*Pause. Neither speaks. Then* RIEL
> *returns to the letters.*]

MARGUERITE

Again the letters, the letters.

RIEL

Marguerite, they are of great importance, these letters. There is great need to think much of what they say.

MARGUERITE

What do they say? You have not told me.

RIEL

This one is from my countrymen in the North-West. From Batoche. The Saskatchewan.

MARGUERITE

The North-West. Batoche. Saskatchewan. Ah, Louis it is no good to me to hear those names.

RIEL

This one is from the good Père André. There is no curé in that country so wise and so well-loved. He says I am to come. Come quickly. He says, [*Reading.*] "Dear Louis Riel. You are the most popular man with all the people here. . . . There will be great disappointment if you do not come. So you see you absolutely must come. . . ."

MARGUERITE

What do they want you for? Why should you go there?

RIEL

Again there is great trouble. Like it was fifteen years ago. My people, again they suffer. They do not get their rights. They wait, they suffer, they send to Ottawa, they beg to have their rights and they get nothing, nothing, only the spittle. . . . [*He illustrates this vigorously.*] And more police, police, police. And now it is enough. They will not take this any more. Now they will fight. They are not—savages. They are not cowards. If to fight is the only way, again they fight they fight . . . and they send for me again to lead them. They send a—deputation.

MARGUERITE

What is it, "deputation"?

RIEL

Some men from my country, my people. They come here today. I look for them. Ah, I have not seen for so long—Gabriel Dumont, Michel Dumas, James **Isbister.** . . .

[MARGUERITE *has been taking in the import of this with growing alarm, she has risen and crossed to him.*] Louis, Louis, men from your country, your people. Your country now is here. Montana, this is your home. And me, our children, *we* are your people. Those men who come—you will not go back with them Louis.

RIEL

God has told me. I have asked God. I have waited fifteen years and now it is God's time. I am to go.

MARGUERITE

You will not go, you will not. Here in Montana you are safe.

RIEL

What is it to be safe? It is not for me. I have known this, always.

MARGUERITE

You have been happy here.

RIEL

Sometimes happy. Now, I am not. Also, to be happy it is not everything.

MARGUERITE

It is everything to me.

RIEL

That is—childish. We are not in this world only to be happy. Marguerite—you know—I told you—I have a mission. I am the Prophet of the New World. God has spoken to me and I must obey.

MARGUERITE

You will not go again to the North-West. You will not. It is trouble for you there—bad trouble. Do you know something, Louis: last night you called out in your sleep. You screamed. Oh Louis it was horrible, that scream. Your hands and face were wet, with sweat. You called out the holy names. I tried to wake you up. I could not. You called out "Cross! a cross! There, on that hill! I am hanging from that cross!" I was scared. I shook you hard. I slapped your hands. The children woke. They cried, to hear you. They were so scared, there in the dark. Poor little Jean Louis. And Marie-Angelique. [*She breaks off, noticing that he is not listening but is gazing off intently, to the left.*] Louis! You do not even listen. What is it, Louis?

RIEL

[*Rising, his face lighting up. He does not avert his gaze from what he is watching off left.*] It is "God's time." Look, they are here.

[*He begins to move off left.*]

MARGUERITE

[*Also on her feet, apprehensive.*] The men. The men from your country.

RIEL

[*Calling and waving his hand as he goes off.*] Gabriel! Gabriel Dumont! Gabriel!

GABRIEL'S VOICE

[*Off left.*] Louis. Louis Riel!

RIEL

Michel Dumas!

[RIEL *goes on, and the names are heard
being called as the men
meet somewhere, off.*]

MARGUERITE

[*As he moves off.*] Louis! The children! I will bring the children. [*She turns to hurry off right, calling to the children.*] Jean Louis! Marie-Angelique!

SCENE 2   *An Open Place in Saskatchewan*

*Tom-toms are heard, at first at some little distance,
but coming closer and beating ever a little faster as
this scene continues. A spot, dimmed, picks out a few
men—they are half-breeds, settlers, Indians, excitedly
grouped down left. They gather round one who has a
paper he is about to read, peering at it, perhaps by a
lantern point of light. There is a tense, conspiritorial
feeling about everything.*

ALL

[*A general whispering.*] Riel. Riel is here, Louis Riel.

THE ONE WITH THE PAPER

It is from him. [*Reads.*] "To the Half-breeds. To the
Indians. From Louis David Riel. Exovede. Dear Brothers. Dear Relatives. It is the time. Justice commands us
to take up arms. Seize all stores. Stop the police and
take their arms. If possible do not kill. Do not molest
or ill-treat anyone. But fear not . . . take arms and
come . . . quickly."

> [*The dimmed spot on this group fades out as a
> dimmed spot comes up on similar small group
> down right. The undercurrent of the whispers—
> "Riel. Riel is here."—is maintained
> continuously between the readings
> from* RIEL'S *messages.*]

SCENE 3 *Another Open Place in*
Saskatchewan

HALF-BREED WITH THE PAPER

[*Reading.*] "Justice commands us to take up arms.
Rise. Face the enemy. Seize all stores, all powder, shot
and cartridges. Join us quickly for the sake of God,
under the keeping of Jesus Christ, the Holy Virgin,
St. Joseph and St. Jean Baptiste. Signed. Louis David
Riel. Exovede."

SCENE 4 *Church at Batoche*

An altar with a monstrance and crucifix. Before the altar RIEL *and the* PRIEST *are in altercation.* RIEL *now wears an oddly assorted quasi-clerical outfit: a black jacket and a purple waistcoat on which hangs a large cross.*

PRIEST

Louis Riel, even at this last moment, before it is too late. I beg you. Lay aside your arms. Do not persist in this blind folly.

RIEL

It is not blind folly.

PRIEST

It is monstrous madness. And evil.

RIEL

It is certainly not evil.

PRIEST

I say it is. It is against the Church. Against religion.

RIEL

No, Father, no.

PRIEST

Armed rebellion! Disobedience to authority!

RIEL

It is obedience, to *the* authority above all authorities— God.

PRIEST

What are you presuming to say?

RIEL

God has told me to fight, and I obey.

PRIEST

That is blasphemy! Rank blasphemy! You cannot understand what you have said.

RIEL

I understand what God has said—to me—directly.

PRIEST

Louis Riel I warn you! You are being deluded. By the enemy of your soul.

RIEL

Deluded?

PRIEST

Yes. Into mistaking the promptings of your own arrogant will and monstrous vanity for the voice of God.

RIEL

[*Coolly.*] This is what they always say. They said it to many Protestants: Protestant martyrs.

PRIEST

Protestants! A Protestant! Possibly a martyr!

RIEL

Father, I wish only to do God's bidding. If for that you call me Protestant [*He shrugs.*] . . . call me Protestant! God bids me lead the people and go forward to this battle without fear.

PRIEST

[*Crying out against it.*] Oh! Oh the pride! the vanity! The blind stubborn will!

RIEL

[*Sharply.*] Father has God ever spoken to you?

PRIEST

What!

RIEL

I mean direct to you, yourself?

PRIEST

I am a priest of the Church. . . .

RIEL

Are you an honest priest?

PRIEST

How dare you!

RIEL

Oh it is not for sarcasm. Honesty is hard, even in religion.

PRIEST

Go on. Instruct me in religion.

RIEL

Or maybe specially hard in religion. For you must know if God speaks direct to anyone there is no mistaking his voice for the promptings of pride or vanity.

PRIEST

When you have quite finished instructing me. . . .

RIEL

No! It is no good! You *will* not see!

PRIEST

What have you come here for? [*Armed half-breeds enter, cross themselves, genuflect and move up toward the altar.*] Why are these men here, carrying arms?

RIEL

To get the Church's blessing on our arms!

PRIEST

There will be no blessing.

RIEL

Today we go into battle.

PRIEST

The Church does not approve.

RIEL

We are facing death.

PRIEST

The Church forbids it. Whoever fires a shot commits a sin.

> [*Half-breeds begin to waver.* RIEL *catches roughly at the* PRIEST's *cassock and pulls it.*]

PRIEST

What are you doing?

RIEL

I think beneath your cassock I might see—an angel. One of Satan's brood. Or Satan himself. . . .

> [*The* PRIEST *cries out and the half-breeds cower and back away.* RIEL *turns on them in fury.*]

RIEL

Stay! Come forward here! Why do you fear this man!
[*Turning again on the* PRIEST.] This man's a traitor—
traitor-priest! Scourge him from this temple he pol-
lutes!

PRIEST

[*To the half-breeds.*] Be warned, all of you! The sacraments will be refused to any man who fires a shot!

RIEL

Away with him! I will give the sacraments myself! I
am God's servant too!

PRIEST

Evil man! Louis Riel—now by the power conferred
on me. . . .

RIEL

Conferred by Satan. The Satan that sits in Rome! On
the Pope's throne! The Anti-Christ!

PRIEST

I name you heretic, arch-heretic!

RIEL

I name you traitor, arch-traitor to the people here. Oh
yes! Hold up your holy hands to heaven! Soiled hands!
Soiled by your treachery! [*To the half-breeds.*] My
brothers, this is true! This priest conspired against us
with the enemy. I have information that he told the
enemy what plans we have, what arms, what stores,
how many of us! Now he forbids us to go on, to fight.
He would withhold the sacraments! But he will not!
He will not! You will receive God into your mouths by
my own hand! [*An afterthought.*] If God is in the
wafer which he is not.

> [*The* PRIEST, *horrified, takes the
> monstrance from the altar and carries
> it off. Some half-breeds move to stop
> him but* RIEL *prevents them.*]

RIEL

Let him go! God is still here with us as well as in that
gilded box! [*He seizes the crucifix from the altar and
holds it up.*] He will go with us to the battle!

PRIEST

[*Turning to shout a malediction as he leaves.*] God
has forsaken you Louis Riel! All now will fail you!
You will be humbled now! Your punishment is sure!

Listen, my brothers, my dear relatives in Jesus Christ!
Do not let that man's words make you afraid. God is
with us. It is God's time to strike the enemy. [*Tom-
toms are heard again, far off, but coming closer as the
scene proceeds.*] God sent the herds of buffalo grazing
on the plains to bless our forebears, in abundance
never-failing!   Marvellous   as   manna   falling   from
heaven! We failed in gratefulness to God. For this our
land was taken from us, a penance for our sins. But
now, that is finished! Now, when we ask justice in our
poverty and suffering, the Government at Ottawa will
no longer put us off with lies. Lies lies lies! And always
more police, more police, no answer but police! [*Angry
mutterings against the police.*] They are all round our
woods. Gathering round us now and closing in. They
are well-armed. But do not fear their firearms who can
destroy our bodies only. It is appropriate we go to
meet them from this Church [*Lifting the crucifix
aloft.*] for we will take God with us. Now—to the rifle
pits. Make your peace with God. Obey him. Ask him
to be among us and to give us victory!

[*Cries of: "Victoire! Vive Riel! God
with us! God with us!" as the rally
gathers behind* RIEL *who, holding the crucifix
aloft, is leading them off. In the general
stir, the Tom-toms are heard again.*]

SCENE 5   *Outside Riel's House, Batoche*

MARGUERITE, *distracted with anxiety, listens to the firing of volley and counter-volley in the distance. There are sounds of a stir nearby.*

MARGUERITE

God is with us. With Louis. We must win. Louis must win. There are many against us but he must win, he must win.

> [*Through the near-by stir rises the sound of lamenting.*]

MARGUERITE

What is that? What is that now? The women crying? What do they say? [*She listens and what she hears confirms her fears.*] Oh Mary ever blessed! Oh do not forsake him now! Help him now! Help him St. Joseph! Joseph most just, most chaste, most prudent, look to him now! Defend him! Pray for him!

VOICES OF LAMENTING WOMEN

Oi, oi, oi!

MARGUERITE

It is lost.

> [WOMAN *comes in. She does not address herself to* MARGUERITE *but laments.*]

WOMAN

Our men they run. They fall down. Maxime. Baptiste. Dead. Many are dead!

MARGUERITE

My Louis?

WOMAN

Gabriel was very brave but he could not! Old man Ouelette, he would not leave the pits, he would not save himself, and he is dead. Pierre, he too! Oh Pierre! Oh Pierriche! The blood poured out! Pierriche, he died ! And Jimus! I saw the horse tramp on his face! Oh Jesu!

MARGUERITE

But Louis, Louis, is there no news of Louis?

WOMAN

[*Out of her daze.*] What? What did you say?

MARGUERITE

Louis?

WOMAN

Louis. No. No. He is gone.

> [*Distant rifle-fire and tom-toms have
> dwindled to nothing.*]

MARGUERITE

[*In dead silence.*] Gone!

WOMAN

Into the woods. They run after him into the woods to catch him! Many police run after him.

MARGUERITE

Oh Louis! You will be taken! This time you will be taken!

SCENE 6 *Tent of General Middleton*

A table and chair. A stool nearby. MIDDLETON *sits at the table in his uniform greatcoat. Scout* ARMSTRONG *approaches and salutes.*

MIDDLETON
Yes, Armstrong?

ARMSTRONG
Riel is here, General.

MIDDLETON
Ah! Bravo! Got him here safely, eh?

ARMSTRONG
Just managed it, but only just.

MIDDLETON
Deuced clever of you!

ARMSTRONG
Did take some cunning. Lots of the boys rearing to get at him. Calling him, "Son of a bitch. Goddam son of a bitch." *Et*cetera!

MIDDLETON
Did Riel himself give trouble?

ARMSTRONG
Couldn't have been less trouble. Meek as a lamb.

MIDDLETON
You don't say! All that noise, but—soft inside?

ARMSTRONG
He's—kinda simple.

MIDDLETON

Foxing?

ARMSTRONG

Couldn't be sure. *Seems* a decent, friendly sort. Got to like him.

MIDDLETON

Well, well. Great thing is you haltered him! Got him here, sound of wind and limb.

ARMSTRONG

Not so sound.

MIDDLETON

What's the matter with him?

ARMSTRONG

Looks miserable. Down in the mouth.

MIDDLETON

Well, in the circumstances—just been thoroughly walloped hasn't he? Hardly expect him to be cock-a-hoop!

ARMSTRONG

No. But as well—pretty cold now here, nights, General! Not much vittals hanging on trees! Poor guy's been drifting around. . . .

MIDDLETON

Ah! Ah, yes, to-be-sure-to-be-sure! Have some hot food brought for him. And, eh . . . fetch one of my greatcoats will you, Armstrong. Must look after him now. After all—eight thousand men, five million dollars out of Canadian pockets to get him here! Prize prisoner!

ARMSTRONG

Prisoner's not what he thinks he is.

MIDDLETON

What? What's that?

ARMSTRONG

He thinks he's here to talk.

MIDDLETON

Talk?

ARMSTRONG

Terms—for an armistice.

MIDDLETON

Armistice! Bless me! [*A loud, mirthless ejaculation.*] Hach! Must be right, all we've heard of him. Must be mad! Well-well-well-well! [*Thinks a moment.*] Well, poor fella, bring him in, bring him in.

[ARMSTRONG *salutes and goes.*]

MIDDLETON

Armistice? Terms? What's he up to? [*He reflects, takes out and examines his pistol.*] Some funny game? Knows he's walloped, surely? Or can't admit? One of these blokes who can't admit? Tiresome! Tiresome fools! Deuce take them!

[ARMSTRONG *brings* RIEL, *who still wears his quasi-clerical outfit—black coat, purple waistcoat with dangling pendant cross. He is bedraggled, dejected, very tired.*]

ARMSTRONG

General, this is Mr. Riel.

[RIEL *bows deeply.* MIDDLETON *rises and shakes hands with him.* ARMSTRONG *retires.*]

MIDDLETON

I hoped we might meet.

RIEL

It was also my hope, but not in these circumstances.

MIDDLETON

H'm! Quite! Quite! [*Moves stool near* RIEL.] Pray be seated.

RIEL

[*Gratefully sitting.*] I thank you. You are kind, General.

MIDDLETON

Not at all, not at all. You've been on the stretch—quite an innings!

RIEL

I had hoped we might have a—little talk.

MIDDLETON

Oh! Indeed!

RIEL

I gave myself up, with that hope. I asked for safe conduct to come here, to tell you the just demands and grievances of my people.

MIDDLETON

Why? What on earth for? Why tell *me*?

RIEL

If you would grant an armistice. . . .

MIDDLETON

Look here, you can't be serious.

RIEL

If there is anything serious in life or death it is most serious that my people's just demands be weighed in Ottawa. An armistice would give time. . . .

MIDDLETON

Out of the question. In fact, preposterous!

RIEL

The grievances of my people. . . .

MIDDLETON

Not my concern. Now, Mr. Riel. . . .

RIEL

If you would do me the honour to let me tell what the North-West is fighting for. . . .

MIDDLETON

My dear good man, the North-West isn't fighting for anything, now. The fighting's over. Surely you understand! It's over. And as for you. . . . Forgive me—you are under arrest.

RIEL

[*He begins to rise.*] I came as emissary.

MIDDLETON

Nonsense! Pray remain seated. [RIEL *hesitates, seems bewildered.*] I am not prepared to. . . .

RIEL

General, as emissary I request, I *demand.* . . .

MIDDLETON

You are being insolent. [*Peremptorily.*] Sit down, sir!

RIEL

[*Sitting, reluctantly.*] I was mistaken in coming here.

MIDDLETON

You had no choice.

RIEL

It is not true, no choice.

MIDDLETON

Mr. Riel. . . .

There were horses saddled and waiting for me to take
me across the border, back to Montana. Gabriel Dumont and Napoleon Nault my cousin had horses and
they begged me to go, with them. I could not. I had
promised God, and my people, and I could not fail
them. I had still to fight for them. I believed you
would protect me till my people's wrongs were
weighed in Ottawa. . . .

MIDDLETON

Mr. Riel, I have every sympathy. But this is not the
place. . . .

RIEL

Then, you will permit me, I will go to Ottawa. . . .

MIDDLETON

No, sir. Certainly not. You stay here. Sorry, but you
are my prisoner. I shall be sending you, in custody,
to Regina. You will stand trial.

RIEL

Prisoner. Trial.

MIDDLETON

You will be tried for treachery to the legal government.

RIEL

They would not answer our petitions. We had to fight.
What else could we do?

MIDDLETON

You thought your half-breeds—a few hundred un-
trained half-breeds and Indians could defeat the whole
of Canada, and Britain herself as well?

RIEL

I thought only if we showed strength of purpose and
would fight, even so monstrously unequal and unfair
a fight. . . .

MIDDLETON

Steady, my good man, steady. Don't harangue me.
I'm not a public meeting.

RIEL

I thought those politicians there in Ottawa at last
would have to listen and deal honourably with us. . . .
[Bitterly.] Not look at each other, oh so sly, and wink
and smile, and file our petitions away for ever. I
thought. . . .

MIDDLETON

Oh, look here, look here. . . .

RIEL

Pardon. You may not know these men. You are a soldier. Those politicians! Dishonest! The sins of the whole world are on their heads. My people here in the North-West, all, all, and not the Métis only. . . .

MIDDLETON

No doubt, no doubt, but. . . .

RIEL

Métis and whites, all have grievances, foul, festering, suppurating sores of grievance that *smell,* and poison the body of society!

MIDDLETON

Spare me, pray, spare me more. You may tell the Court. All this. Pour it all out in Court. 'Twill do you good, I'm sure—"cleanse your bosom of such perilous stuff."

RIEL

[*Hushed, uplifted and lapsed, as if he has had an illumination.*] Yes! Yes!

MIDDLETON

"Such?" "Much?" *Much* perilous stuff? Oh bother! Comes to the same thing. Bother the Bard!

RIEL

General. . . .

MIDDLETON

What? What now?

RIEL

A light—breaks! God *is* with me! He sent me to you. *This* is his plan! His Divine Providence opens a way for me to tell our story where all Canada, all the world will hear. [*He closes his eyes. Prays.*] Oh my Father I thank thee. . . .

MIDDLETON

H'm! H'm! Well now! Well, if that's all right, if that's agreed.

RIEL

[*Looking around at* MIDDLETON, *as if still lapsed in vision.*] May I be worthy. St. Joseph, help me to be worthy when I come to that Court.

[*He suddenly sways and slumps down on the stool.*]

MIDDLETON

Mr. Riel!

RIEL

[*With an effort.*] Forgive me. I am weary. Very weary.

MIDDLETON

Poor man, no wonder no wonder! [*Brightly.*] But—we can do something about that!

> [ARMSTRONG *has come to the tent with hot rations,*
> *with one of* MIDDLETON's *military greatcoats*
> *over his arm.* MIDDLETON *indicates to him to set*
> *down the rations, and winks covertly*
> *his half-amused contempt of* RIEL's *condition.*
> *Then, quietly, to* ARMSTRONG.]

MIDDLETON

Rum.

ARMSTRONG

Rum?

MIDDLETON

Rum. [*They exchange looks.* ARMSTRONG *grimaces and goes out.* MIDDLETON *puts his hand on* RIEL's *shoulder. Kindly.*] Come now. Come. A little food. A little warmth. Good sleep. Can work wonders. [*He holds his greatcoat for* RIEL.] First, this. Feel better in this.

SCENE 7   *Courtroom, Regina*

The VOICE OF THE CLERK *of the Court is heard.*

VOICE OF THE CLERK
    Oyez, oyez, oyez!

> [*He enters, down right, gowned and holding papers in his hand. As he enters he is speaking.*]

CLERK
    That the said Louis Riel . . . not regarding the duty
    of his allegiance to our sovereign Lady the Queen,
    nor having the fear of God in his heart, but being
    moved and seduced by the instigation of the Devil as
    a false traitor against our said Lady the Queen, here
    stands charged before my lord the Queen's Justice.' . . .
    [*While the* CLERK *has been speaking, four separate
    areas have been spot-lighted. In Spot One, down left,*
    JUDGE RICHARDSON *is standing before the raised seat
    which is the "bench." In Spot Two, up left centre,*
    RIEL *stands behind a rail which is the dock. Spot
    Three, down right of centre, and Spot Four, down
    right, are for the time-being unoccupied. In the unlit
    area, up right, stand, in separate groups, the* SIX JURY-
    MEN, CROWN *and* DEFENCE COUNSEL, WITNESSES, *and
    the* PUBLIC. *The* CLERK *now moves to vicinity of the
    "bench." An usher's "knock-knock" is heard.*]

CLERK
    Order! Order!

> [JUDGE RICHARDSON *bows deeply to the Court and
> sits down. All others remain standing.*]

CLERK

[*Gabbling it off rapidly.*] Oyez oyez oyez all persons having business with my lord the Queen's Justice draw near and give attention and you shall be heard God save the Queen.

[*All present, except* RIEL, *sit down.*]

JUDGE

[*As to himself, consulting his papers.*] Queen versus Riel. High treason. [*Calls.*] Louis Riel. [RIEL *bows deeply and remains standing.*] Counsel for the Crown. [*The* COUNSEL *for the Crown steps forward into Spot Three, bows to the* JUDGE *and retires.*] Counsel for the defence. [*The* COUNSEL *for the defence steps forward into Spot Three, bows to the* JUDGE *and retires.*] Arraign the prisoner.

CLERK

[*Rising from his position below the "bench."*] On this the sixth day of July in the year of our Lord, 1885, at the town of Regina, Louis Riel, you stand charged on oath that with divers other false traitors armed and arrayed in a warlike manner, you did levy and make war against our Lady the Queen, and did maliciously and traitorously attempt by force of arms to destroy the Constitution and Government of the Realm ... and to depose our said Lady the Queen from the style honour and kingly name of the Imperial Crown of the Realm to the evil example of others in like case offending. Louis Riel, are you guilty or not guilty?

RIEL

I have the honour to answer the Court I am not guilty.

CLERK

You may sit down.

[RIEL *bows and sits down. The* JUDGE *nods to the* CROWN ATTORNEY, *who enters Spot Three.*]

JUDGE

Proceed.

CROWN

The jury assembled here must pass judgment in the most serious trial that has ever taken place in Canada. In the presence of witnesses the prisoner stated that in one week the Government police would be wiped out of existence. A few days later he told another witness that the rebellion had commenced; that he had been waiting fifteen years to get this opportunity. He wrote and signed an ultimatum to Major Crozier of the North-West Mounted Police in which he stated:

"We intend to commence a war of extermination upon all who have shown themselves hostile to our rights." I think you will be satisfied before this case is over that this matter is brought about by the personal vanity of the man on trial. I would like to call as witness Major General Frederick Middleton.

[MIDDLETON *enters Spot Four. The oath in brief form may be taken by successive witnesses.*]

CROWN

General Middleton, you commanded the Canadian Militia in its campaign against the rebels at Batoche and Duck Lake?

MIDDLETON

Yes, that is correct.

CROWN

Did you at any time see the prisoner in the field of battle?

MIDDLETON

I did. At Duck Lake. Although he did not appear to be armed, he led a charge on horseback and shouted encouragement to his troops.

CROWN

Tell us what happened at Batoche.

MIDDLETON

There was some severe fighting. Our troops encountered unexpectedly stiff opposition. The enemy were so skilfully concealed in rifle-pits behind thick cover that we could neither see them nor get at them. Their commander, one Gabriel Dumont—who, I understand, was responsible for the actual military operations—showed uncommon skill, as well as a thorough grasp of all the tricks and cunning associated with Indian methods of so-called warfare.

CROWN

Can you say what part in all this, if any, was played by the prisoner.

MIDDLETON

He seems to have been the ringleader. He managed to inspire his men with almost fanatical bravery and tenacity. We were unable to dislodge them until we could bring into play the superior fire-power of our Gatling gun. That made short work of 'em. Got 'em on the run. Soon they dispersed altogether, and I sent out scouts to search the woods as far as Batoche. Scouts

Howrie and Armstrong came upon the prisoner wandering in the woods. He asked them for safe conduct. To be brought to me with the purpose, he said, of discussing terms. When he reached my tent he said he had come to ask for an armistice, to have the just demands and grievances of his people seriously weighed by Ottawa. I told him the people's demands and grievances weren't my affair. And that he would be taken in custody to Regina, where he'd have a chance to put his case before a court of law. And— well—here we are.

CROWN

In what capacity did he present himself to you, with this absurd request for an armistice?

MIDDLETON

He said he was leader of the Métis.

CROWN

Did he speak to you on religious subjects?

MIDDLETON

Oh yes. From the first moment. Later, he spoke often of religion. He said the saints had talked to him. That visions had been vouchsafed to him. He told me St. Peter had appeared to him, in the Church of St. James at Washington, District of Columbia. He said St. Peter had ordered him to undertake his mission.

CROWN

His mission?

MIDDLETON

To lead the people of the North-West. He said a Bishop, or Archbishop, called Bourget, I think, had already told him he had a mission. He seemed to have Mission on the brain. It bored me. I remember thinking, Oh confound him, he's always bothering about the saints and his mission and religion. He's anxious I should know about his religion. I noticed that when any conversation reached a point where he wanted to evade or gain time to answer—he immediately turned to religious matters.

CROWN

Ah! He used his ideas on religion in that way?

MIDDLETON

I so regarded it.

CROWN

Tell us any of the views he expressed on religion.

MIDDLETON

He spoke about Rome and the Pope. He wanted the government of the Church to be located not in Rome but here, in the new world, in Canada.

CROWN

The Vatican in Canada?

MIDDLETON

Yes. He told me he thought Rome was all wrong and corrupt, and that the priests were narrow-minded and had interfered too much with the people. And others of his ideas were excessively good.

CROWN

What were they?

MIDDLETON

He thought that religion should be based on humanity and morality and charity. His view of hell was that God's mercy was too great to be sinned away by anyone in the short time he had to live. Also he wanted to purge the Christian Church of its relics of paganism —such as the names of the days of the week.

CROWN

He wanted to give new names to the days of the week?

MIDDLETON

Yes, instead of the present pagan names.

CROWN

During all your interviews with him did you see anything to indicate unsoundness of mind?

MIDDLETON

On the contrary, I should say he was a man of rather acute intellect; in fact, deucedly clever.

CROWN

And the idea of mental aberration never occured to you?

MIDDLETON

I believe it was put on—for a purpose.

CROWN

Thank you.

> [*The* CROWN *gives place in Spot Three to the* DEFENCE.]

DEFENCE

What experience have you had in dealing with people of unsound mind?

MIDDLETON

None at all.

DEFENCE

But you think yourself qualified to give an opinion as to sanity?

MIDDLETON

Not a medical opinion. But I think that in living with him several days I would know if I was living with a lunatic.

DEFENCE

Are you aware that medical experts say it takes four months to detect insanity in many cases?

MIDDLETON

Living with him it would be different.

DEFENCE

Have you seen any document signed by the prisoner?

MIDDLETON

Yes.

DEFENCE

Was there anything peculiar in the manner of the signature?

MIDDLETON

The signature was sometimes Louis Riel and sometimes Louis David Riel. I understand he included David to identify himself with the Biblical hero—the boy who slew the giant with a sling shot.

JUDGE

Was this told you by Riel himself?

MIDDLETON

No, your honour.

DEFENCE

Any other peculiarity you observed about his signature?

MIDDLETON

The word exovede.

DEFENCE

Exovede?

MIDDLETON

It frequently appeared after his name. He told me he invented it—from the Latin words, *ex*, from, and *ovile*, flock. From the flock. He said he used it to show he was assuming no authority except as one of the flock, an ordinary member of society. He said that his Council, being composed of exovedes, was to be called, exovedate.

DEFENCE

[*With careful point.*] And in all this—you see no indication whatever of mental aberration?

MIDDLETON

As I said, I think he put it all on—for a purpose.

DEFENCE

Thank you.

[MIDDLETON *retires. The* DEFENCE *steps out of Spot Three.*]

CLERK

Charles Nolin.

[NOLIN *enters Spot Four. The* CROWN *enters Spot Three.*]

CROWN

You know the prisoner?

NOLIN

He is my cousin.

CROWN

You have frequently seen him since he returned from Montana?

NOLIN

When he returned he was a guest in my house for several weeks.

CROWN

Did he talk to you about his ideas and plans?

NOLIN

He never stopped talking about them.

CROWN

Tell us something of what he said.

NOLIN

He said he was sending out messengers all over the country with secret messages to rouse the Indians and half-breeds. Calling them to come and help. He said that together we could defeat the police and militia and bring Canada to her knees. He said he had plans to bring foreign armies here, to drive out Canada and take possession of Manitoba and the North-West for the half-breeds and Indians. He said if we didn't drive out or destroy the white men we would be over-run and driven out or destroyed ourselves. He said the white men from the east would keep on swarming in to grab our lands. And that we would soon be no better than so many hungry, mangy coyotes to be hunted and shot at. We were to go on living our own kind of life, respecting and keeping up our own old customs and laws, and fighting for that to the death; or be despised and pushed aside and go down, down, down till we were lost.

CROWN

He seriously thought that a scattering of half-breeds and Indians had a right, and duty, to fence off these vast empty lands against the spread of population from all the rest of the over-crowded world?

NOLIN

He said what was ours was ours and we should fight and fight to hold it. Any man who wouldn't take up arms and fight to hold it was a traitor. He said we were to rise in arms. He had asked God and God had told him. He had waited fifteen years for God to tell him. And God had told him. It was God's time. We were to rise in arms.

CROWN

Did you believe this?

NOLIN

No.

CROWN

But many did?

NOLIN

They thought he was a prophet. He played on this. He could do what he liked with them. They were ready to die for him.

CROWN

And many of them did?

NOLIN

Yes. There was much bloodshed and great misery.

CROWN

Would it be true to say that prisoner was the chief instigator of this rising in arms?

NOLIN

He was the one that roused the people to get together and fight; but Gabriel Dumont was the one that planned and led the fighting here, like Ambroise Lépine did fifteen years ago at Fort Garry.

CROWN

But prisoner was the one who roused them to fight?

NOLIN

Without him it would not have happened. It might have flared up but it would have fizzled out.

CROWN

One last question. When the fighting started did prisoner himself take any active part in it?

NOLIN

He was the one that went about the rifle-pits giving the order to fire.

[*The* CROWN *gives place to the* DEFENCE.]

DEFENCE

Prisoner, you say, is your cousin?

NOLIN

Yes.

DEFENCE

You have—or had—great affection and admiration for him?

NOLIN

We were on friendly terms.

DEFENCE

But you did admire him?

NOLIN

I thought he was—clever—a cut above the rest of us.

DEFENCE

Were you ever envious or jealous of his cleverness.

NOLIN

No.

DEFENCE

You have mentioned the trouble at Fort Garry. Is it true that there, as here again, you were with your cousin and his cause at first, and later decided to desert them?

NOLIN

I had to be with him at first. It was the only way to save my life. I did not think he would fight. I did not want to fight.

[*During the examination of this witness,* RIEL *shows signs of exasperation and resentment.*]

DEFENCE

When you thought he would not fight you were with him to save your life. When you thought he would fight, and might be defeated, you again decided to save your life?

NOLIN

I did not want to fight, there or here. Here, when I'd had enough, he had me arrested and court-martialled. I was condemned to death, but reprieved. Then I escaped.

DEFENCE

And now you are here to give evidence against him! You have said that at the rifle-pits he gave orders to fire. Did he himself fire?

NOLIN

He had no rifle. He was always afraid of fire-arms. When the shooting started he went about carrying a crucifix.

DEFENCE

What for? What did he do with the crucifix?

NOLIN

When a volley was fired by the police and militia he lifted up the crucifix and gave the order to fire in return. He said: "In the name of God the Father who created us, reply to that!" Next time it would be: "In the name of Jesus Christ who redeemed us, reply to that!" Next it would be: "In the name of the Holy Ghost who sanctifies us, reply to that!" And so on, calling on the saints one after another.

DEFENCE

Did this strike you as in any way unusual or peculiar?

NOLIN

He was always trying to make out there was something out of the ordinary about him. That he was a prophet. Speaking for God. He even dressed up sometimes like a sort of priest—in a black suit with a purple waistcoat and a big cross hanging on his front.

DEFENCE

Did *that* strike you as indicating anything not quite normal in his mentality?

NOLIN

I think he knew what he was doing.

[RIEL, *unable to restrain himself any longer, suddenly rises.*]

RIEL

Your Honour, would you permit me a little while to. . . .

JUDGE

[*Surprised and a little flustered.*] Eh? What?

RIEL

I have some questions. . . .

JUDGE

At the proper time. You will be given every opportunity.

RIEL

Is there any legal way that I could be allowed to speak? To ask some questions?

JUDGE

You should suggest any questions to your own Counsel.

RIEL

Do you allow me to speak? I have some observations, some questions to ask this witness. . . .

DEFENCE

[*Interrupting.*] I don't think this is the proper time, your Honour.

RIEL

Before this man leaves the witness box. . . .

JUDGE

I agree it is not the proper time.

[RIEL *reluctantly sits down.*]

DEFENCE

I think it is necessary that the prisoner should thoroughly understand that anything that is done in his behalf in this case must be done through me.

JUDGE

The statute of High Treason states that the prisoner can defend himself personally or by counsel.

DEFENCE

But after counsel has been accepted. . . .

RIEL

[*Rising again.*] Your Honour, this case comes to be extraordinary. The Crown are trying to show that I am guilty. It is their duty. My Counsel, my good friends and lawyers, whom I respect, are trying to show that I am insane. It is their line of defence. I reject it. I indignantly deny that I am insane. I am not insane! I declare. . . .

JUDGE

Now you must stop.

RIEL

The chance to ask important questions of witness is slipping by. My good Counsel does not know what questions to ask because he does not know this man and because he is from Quebec and does not understand our ways out here. . . .

JUDGE

I have said you must stop. Now stop at once.

RIEL

I will stop and obey your Court.

CROWN

[*Rising, smiling and soothing.*] Your Honour, the prosecution does not object to the prisoner putting questions to witnesses.

DEFENCE

[*Becoming angry.*] Your Honour, the prisoner is actually obstructing the proper management of his case and he must not be allowed to interfere in it.

JUDGE

Isn't that a matter between yourself and your client?

DEFENCE

I don't pretend to argue with the Court, but if I am to continue the case the prisoner must be made to abandon his attitude.

RIEL

[*Again rising.*] I cannot abandon my dignity. Here I have to defend myself against the accusation of high treason. Or I have to allow the plea that I am insane and consent to the animal life of an asylum. I don't care much about animal life if I am not allowed to carry with it the moral existence of an intellectual being.

JUDGE

[*Peremptorily.*] Now stop.

RIEL

[*Beaten. He sits down.*] Yes, your Honour.

JUDGE

[*To the* DEFENCE.] Proceed.

DEFENCE

[*To* NOLIN.] You may go. [*To the* CLERK.] Call Father André.

CLERK

Father Alexis André.

[Father ANDRE *enters Spot Four.*
He is a noticeably unkempt bearded
man in a greasy cassock.]

DEFENCE

What is your name in religion?

ANDRE

Alexis André, Oblat.

DEFENCE

Since how long have you been in this country?

ANDRE

Since 1865 in The Saskatchewan.

DEFENCE

You know of the political activities of the population?

ANDRE

I do.

DEFENCE

Do you know of petitions and resolutions being sent to
the Federal Government?

ANDRE

Yes.

DEFENCE

Did these petitions and resolutions—adopted at public
meetings and sent to the Government—have any result?

ANDRE

The continual silence or evasions of the Government
produced great dissatisfaction, and drove the people
to think their only hope lay in resort to force. And
I. . . .

[The COUNSEL *for the* CROWN
intervenes, coming into the spot
with the DEFENCE.*]*

CROWN

[To the JUDGE.*]* I must object to this class of question.
My learned friend has opened a case of treason justified only by the insanity of the prisoner, and he is now
seeking to justify armed rebellion for the redress of
their grievances.

JUDGE

Which is like trying the Government.

CROWN

And that isn't open to any one on trial for high treason. [*Withdraws.*]

DEFENCE

[*To the* JUDGE.] I don't want to justify the rebellion. I want to show the state of things in the country, and that the prisoner was justified in coming back across the border from Montana.

JUDGE

That, I think, is not questioned.

DEFENCE

[*He bows to the* JUDGE, *and turns again to the* WIT- NESS.] You have had occasion to meet the prisoner between July 1884 and the time of the rebellion?

ANDRE

Yes.

DEFENCE

Have you spoken to him on politics and religion?

ANDRE

Frequently.

DEFENCE

Did he speak in a sensible manner?

ANDRE

Not on politics and religion. On these subjects he did not have his intelligence of mind. I want to state a fact to the Court regarding the prisoner. You know the life of that man affected us during a certain time.

DEFENCE

In what way?

ANDRE

He was a fervent Catholic, attending to his religious duties. But he stated things that frightened the priests. And he was subject to violent outbursts in which he would flout the authority and holy office of the priests. It is true that when the rebellious and hot-tempered mood had passed he would appear sad and contrite. He would then outdo himself in being extravagantly apologetic and polite, even abasing himself. Once, all the priests met together to decide if the man could be allowed to continue in his religious duties. They unanimously decided that, on questions of religion and politics, there was no way of explaining his conduct except that he was insane.

Insane?

ANDRE

Insane.

[The CROWN *replaces the* DEFENCE
in Spot Three.]

CROWN

You say the prisoner made statements that frightened
the priests. What statements?

ANDRE

He wanted to change the Mass and the liturgy, the
ceremonies and the symbols. He thought only the first
person in the Trinity was God, and he did not admit
the doctrine of the Divine Presence. God was not
present in the Host according to him, but only an
ordinary man six feet high.

CROWN

Do you deny that a man may be a great reformer of
religious questions without being a fool?

ANDRE

I do not deny history.

CROWN

Is it not a fact that the half-breeds are extremely religious, and that religion has a great influence on them?

ANDRE

Yes. It was just because he was so religious and appeared so devout that he exercised such a great influence on them.

CROWN

He was at pains to appear devout to the half-breeds?

ANDRE

I did not say "he was at pains."

CROWN

But you do say he appeared devout to the half-breeds?

ANDRE

Yes.

CROWN

You heard the evidence of the previous witnesses?

ANDRE

Yes.

CROWN

You heard them give their opinion that prisoner sometimes used religion for a purpose?

ANDRE

I have said that where religion is concerned I believe
the prisoner is of unsound mind.

CROWN

Thank you.

[ANDRE *and the*
CROWN *withdraw.*]

CLERK

François Roy, doctor of medicine.

[DR. ROY *enters Spot Four. The*
DEFENCE *enters Spot Three.*]

DEFENCE

You are a doctor of medicine?

ROY

Yes.

DEFENCE

In the City of Quebec?

ROY

Yes. For a great many years I have been medical
superintendent, and one of the proprietors, of the
lunatic asylum of Beaufort.

DEFENCE

You have made a special study of the diseases of the
brain?

ROY

Yes.

DEFENCE

Were you superintendent of the asylum at Beaufort
in 1875 and 1876?

ROY

Yes.

DEFENCE

In those years did you see the prisoner?

ROY

Many times.

DEFENCE

Where?

ROY

> In the asylum.

DEFENCE

> As a patient?

ROY

> Yes.

DEFENCE

> Was he admitted with all the formalities required by law?

ROY

> Yes.

DEFENCE

> Did you study the mental disease by which the prisoner was afflicted?

ROY

> Yes—megalomania.

DEFENCE

> In a case of this kind, could a casual observer, without medical experience, form an estimate as to the state of the man's mind?

ROY

> Not usually.

DEFENCE

> You were present at the examination of witnesses here today?

ROY

> Yes.

DEFENCE

> You heard their evidence as to the prisoner's views on religion?

ROY

> I did.

DEFENCE

> From what you heard can you say whether he was then of sound mind?

ROY

> I believe he was of unsound mind.

DEFENCE

> Do you believe he was capable or incapable of knowing the nature and quality of the acts which he did?

ROY

I believe he was not master of his acts.

DEFENCE

Will you swear that the man did not know what he was doing, or whether he was contrary to law in reference to his particular delusion?

ROY

That is my belief.

[The DEFENCE *gives place to the* CROWN *in Spot Three.]*

CROWN

Under what name was the prisoner in your asylum?

ROY

Under the name of Larochelle.

CROWN

Did you know that the man was Riel?

ROY

He himself told me so.

CROWN

From what facts in evidence did you say the prisoner was incapable of distinguishing between right and wrong?

ROY

They never could persuade him that his special mission didn't exist.

CROWN

How would you describe his belief in his special mission?

ROY

As an insane delusion.

CROWN

Do you say that any man claiming to be inspired is suffering from an insane delusion, so as not to be able to distinguish between right and wrong?

ROY

It is possible.

CROWN

Does not the whole evidence sustain the theory, that prisoner's claim to a special mission was a skilful fraud?

ROY

There is no evidence of fraud.

CROWN

Do you say the evidence is inconsistent with fraud?

ROY

When the prisoner was under my care. . . .

CROWN

[*Sharply.*] Will you answer my question.

ROY

Put the question another way.

CROWN

[*He pauses. Then, with a glance at the* JUDGE, *he continues.*] If you cannot answer my question, I may as well let you go. You may go.

[ROY *and the* CROWN
withdraw.]

CLERK

Dr. Jukes.

[DR. JUKES *enters Spot Four.*
The CROWN *re-enters Spot Three.*]

CROWN

You are at present the medical officer attached to the Mounted Police force?

JUKES

I am the Senior Surgeon of the Mounted Police.

CROWN

In your medical capacity insane persons come under your observation?

JUKES

Yes.

CROWN

You know the prisoner?

JUKES

Yes.

CROWN

Have you formed an opinion as to his sanity or insanity?

JUKES

I have seen nothing to induce me to believe he is insane.

CROWN

Is he capable of knowing the nature and quality of any act which he would commit, so as to distinguish between right and wrong?

JUKES

Very acutely.

[CROWN *gives place to the* DEFENCE]

DEFENCE

You have heard of the mental disease known as megalomania?

JUKES

Yes.

DEFENCE

What are the symptoms?

JUKES

The patient has delusions, grandiose delusions.

DEFENCE

That he is powerful?

JUKES

Yes.

DEFENCE

A great soldier?

JUKES

Yes.

DEFENCE

A great leader and statesman?

JUKES

Yes.

DEFENCE

That he is identified with some heroic Biblical or other character?

JUKES

Yes.

DEFENCE

That he is a great prophet with a mission divinely inspired?

JUKES

He may be a great anything and everything.

DEFENCE

Do such insane persons believe they are in constant intercourse with God and are directed by him?

JUKES

I have known patients of that kind.

DEFENCE

From the evidence and your own observation you have no doubt that prisoner's conduct is compatible with a perfectly sound mind?

JUKES

I've heard nothing that might not be accounted for by other causes, for instance fraud or deception.

DEFENCE

If it can be proved that a man is labouring under an insane delusion that he was in communication with the Holy Ghost and acting under direct inspiration of God, and was bound to do a certain act, and did it, would he be responsible for that act?

JUKES

Views on that subject are so different, even among the sane. . . . There are men who have held very remarkable views on religion and who have always been declared to be insane—until they gathered great numbers of followers in a new sect—then they became great prophets and great men; Mahomet for instance.

DEFENCE

You think the conduct of Mr. Riel compatible with the conduct of a man like Mahomet?

JUKES

[*Carefully.*] My opinion is, rather, that Mr. Riel is a man of great shrewdness and very great depth, and that he *might* have assumed, for the purpose of maintaining his influence with his followers, more than he really believed.

DEFENCE

That is your impression, doctor?

JUKES

I have thought it *might* be so.

DEFENCE

Are you in a position to say, doctor, on your oath, that this man is not insane?

JUKES

I have never spoken to him on a single subject on which he has spoken irrationally.

DEFENCE

Thank you.

> [JUKES *leaves Spot Four.*
> *The* DEFENCE *steps outside Spot Three.*]

CLERK

Police officer, Bromley-Witheroe.

> [*The* POLICEMAN *enters Spot Four.*
> *The* DEFENCE *re-enters Spot Three.*]

DEFENCE

You are an Englishman?

POLICEMAN

I am.

DEFENCE

And you have had a good education?

POLICEMAN

[*With a deprecating smile.*] Well, it may not be an answer but I *am* a university graduate.

DEFENCE

The prisoner has been in your charge?

POLICEMAN

Yes.

DEFENCE

So you have had ample opportunity to observe him?

POLICEMAN

I have.

DEFENCE

Tell us what you have observed.

POLICEMAN

He occupies the cell next to the guard room in the barracks. His little statue of St. Joseph stands on the table and when he's telling his beads I've noticed that he holds it in his hand and hugs it. His countenance usually displays a calm composure, and his eyes are nearly always bent on the ground as if he were wrapped in contemplation and study.

DEFENCE

Can you tell us more? Anything in his conduct that seemed to you different from that of the other prisoners?

POLICEMAN

He wrote a great deal in a book which he describes as written with buffalo blood.

DEFENCE

With buffalo blood?

POLICEMAN

Yes. I understand it's about himself and what he calls his people, his mission in the North-West. A sort of *apologia pro vita sua.*

DEFENCE

Have you noticed any other peculiarity of conduct?

POLICEMAN

Sometimes in his cell he talks all night.

DEFENCE

To whom?

POLICEMAN

There's no one visible in the cell with him. But he talks as though God were in the cell with him. He speaks intimately, addressing God by name. And sometimes it's one of the Saints. Particularly St. Joseph. He addresses himself frequently as if to the actual presence of St. Joseph.

DEFENCE

And at such times he speaks aloud?

POLICEMAN

Not always. Frequently there's a prolonged, deeply earnest talking in a low voice. A sort of—urgent whispering. But often he talks aloud.

DEFENCE

And continues in this all night?

POLICEMAN

Well, we have to stop him, for the sake of prisoners trying to sleep in neighbouring cells.

DEFENCE

On such occasions did Riel resent being stopped?

POLICEMAN

No. When we spoke to him through the grid he seemed at first not to understand, as if he were still —apart—in some sort of trance or dream. When he did come to, and understood where he was and what we wanted, he would be apologetic and most polite, and would comply.

[DEFENCE *gives place to the* CROWN.]

CROWN

In your observation of the prisoner did you at any time form the opinion you were dealing with a lunatic?

POLICEMAN

If by lunatic you mean. . . .

CROWN

A person of unsound mind.

POLICEMAN

I'm not sure what constitutes soundness of mind.

CROWN

So you will not say that you thought the prisoner insane?

POLICEMAN

No. He seems to me one of those . . . singular persons. . . . [*Suddenly.*] After all people have called Hamlet insane.

CROWN

[*Pouncing.*] Ah, but was not Hamlet "putting an antic disposition on"?

POLICEMAN

Yes.

CROWN

Do you think prisoner was "putting an antic disposition on"?

[*The* POLICEMAN *pauses, uncertain.*]

CROWN

[*Sharply.*] Well, do you?

POLICEMAN

[*Slowly, considering it thoughtfully.*] I have never quite been able to make up my mind.

CROWN

Thank you.

[*The* CROWN *and the* POLICEMAN *withdraw. Spots Three and Four are out. Only* RIEL *and the* JUDGE *are highlighted, in Spot Two and Spot One.*]

CLERK

The prisoner Louis Riel.

[*Rising and bowing gravely.*] Your Honour. Honourable Court. You will have seen by the papers in the hands of the Crown, I am naturally inclined to think of God at the beginning of my actions. I wish, if I do, you will not take it as a mark of insanity, or as a play of insanity. [*He clasps his hands and closes his eyes, and prays, with deep humility and simplicity.*] Oh my God help me through thy grace and the divine influence of Jesus Christ. Bless me. Bless the honourable Court. Bless all who are around me now through the grace of Jesus Christ our Saviour. Change the curiosity of those who are paying attention to me now. Change that curiosity into sympathy for me. Amen. [*He opens his eyes and looks around. Then, not rhetorical, but intimate, tender.*] The day of my birth I was helpless, and my mother took care of me, and I lived. Today although I am a man, I am as helpless before this Court in the Dominion of Canada, and in this world, as I was helpless on the knees of my mother, the day of my birth.

The North-West also is my mother. It is my mother country. And I am sure my mother country will not kill me . . . any more than my mother did, forty years ago when I came into this world. Because, even if I have my faults, she is my mother and will see that I am true, and be full of love for me.

I believe I have a mission. [*The lights begin to dim out, slowly.*] I say humbly that through the grace of God—who is in this box with me—I am the Prophet of the New World.

First I worked to get free institutions for Manitoba. Now—though I was exiled from Manitoba for my pains—they have those institutions, and I am here, hounded, outlawed. . . . [*The stage is now dark.*]

SCENE 8   *Vicinity of Courtroom, Regina*

Down right, a WOMAN *meets the* SHERIFF.

WOMAN
Please, Sheriff, please. . . .

SHERIFF
What is it?

WOMAN
I know Louis Riel. I know him since he was a little
boy. I want to tell the Judge about Louis.

SHERIFF
No, no, no, no, I'm sorry. . . .

WOMAN
They don't understand Louis in there. It is wrong
about him in there. It is not Louis. I know Louis. I
know his mother. I knew his father, too, Jean Louis.
He was for us too, the half-breed people. . . .

SHERIFF
Yes, yes, I'm sorry, but it's quite impossible for me
to. . . . [*She clutches at him imploringly, and he
impatiently casts her off.*] Keep your hands off! Let
go of me!

WOMAN
Don't put me away, please sir please.

SHERIFF
You can't possibly speak to the Judge.

WOMAN

Then the jury. . . .

SHERIFF

Nor any of the jury. Certainly not!

WOMAN

But they are kind men; they will want to know about Louis; they will see I come only to tell the truth for Louis.

SHERIFF

You don't seem to understand. If you try to speak to them. . . .

WOMAN

[*Frantic.*] I must I must. . . .

SHERIFF

[*Sternly.*] Do you want to be sent to jail!

> [*The* POLICEMAN, *walking from the left,*
> *has noticed and overheard, the*
> SHERIFF *by a nod and glance has him take*
> *over. The* SHERIFF *goes briskly on his way off,*
> *left; the* POLICEMAN *takes the* WOMAN's *arm*
> *kindly and leads her off, right.*]

POLICEMAN

It'll be all right with him. He'll be all right. Come now, come. The law is very fair. It's better not to interfere. Better for him.

WOMAN

Not to interfere! His friends that knew him, not to interfere!

SCENE 9 *Courtroom, Regina*

The lights gradually come up on RIEL *nearing the conclusion of his speech.*

RIEL

. . . Petition after petition was sent from the North-West to the Federal Government, and so irresponsible is that Government that in the course of several years, besides doing nothing to satisfy the just claims of the people, they hardly troubled even to reply. All they have done is to send police and more police. That fact indicates absolute lack of responsibility. Insanity of government! Insanity complicated with paralysis. I was called by the people to lead them in their struggle against this insanity. I came. I came back from exile —to help them. And when I was pounced upon by armed police, I answered with arms. That is what is called my crime of high treason, for which they hold me today and for which they would tear me in pieces. If you take the plea of the defence that I am not responsible for my acts, acquit me completely. If you pronounce in favour of the Crown, which contends I am responsible, acquit me all the same. You are perfectly justified in declaring that, having my reason, I acted with sound mind in quarrelling with an insane and irresponsible Government. If there is high treason, it is not mine but theirs—their high treason against the people of the North-West.

JUDGE

[*Wearied.*] Now are you done?

RIEL

If you have the kindness to permit me. . . .

JUDGE

Well, if you must, you must.

RIEL

I am glad the Crown has proved I am the leader of the half-breeds of the North-West. That is important to remember. It means I stand in this dock not as myself only, but as the chosen representative and leader of a whole people—the half-breed people. Can a whole people be guilty of treason? I beg you to think of that. I am their leader—and one day perhaps I will be acknowledged as more than a leader of the half-breeds —as a leader of good in this great country.

All my life I have worked for practical results. If I have succeeded, after my death my children will shake hands with the Protestants. I do not want those evils which exist in Europe to be repeated here. There will be at last a New World. But not in some days or years. It will take hundreds of years.

Yet, now, we make a beginning. We invite to our new world Italians, Poles, Bavarians, Belgians, the Swedes, the Irish, the Jews—all, all are welcome here, provided only they will help us with their work and with their money, and by acknowledging Jesus Christ as the only hope of mankind and the Saviour of the World.

Now by the soil of this great land they have their start to make a nation. Who starts the nations? God. God is the maker of the universe. Our planet is in His hands. All the nations, the tribes, are members of His family. To each as a good Father He gives their inheritance. God cannot create a tribe, a nation, without locating it. We are not birds. We have to walk on the ground. And this is our ground, our country. And we will enrich it. We will cultivate it. This is the genius of civilization. Honourable Court, that is what as a public man, Riel has said. Of this I am guilty. Of the charge against me I am not guilty. I am confident that for this I will not be destroyed.

JUDGE

Is *that* all?

RIEL

Yes, that is all. Except to put my speech under the protection of my God my Saviour. He is the only one who can make it effective. And He will not fail me. If I have been astray, I have been acting not as an impostor but according to my conscience. Your Honour, that is what I have to say. [*He bows gravely to the Court and then kneels down in the dock in silent prayer.*]

CLERK

The jury will retire to consider their verdict.

JUDGE

Adjourned.

CLERK

Court adjourned.

SCENE 10 *Vicinity of Courtroom, Regina*

The CROWN *and* DEFENCE *come walking slowly from the right, discussing the case.*

CROWN

Must congratulate you. A most skilful defence.

DEFENCE

Thank you. But the jury was with you to the last, I'm afraid.

CROWN

Wish I could think so, but I'm not so sure. They showed lots of sympathy for him at times.

DEFENCE

True, true—if only he hadn't squandered it by tiresome verbosity. French-Canadians will still demand to know why he was tried by an exclusively Anglo-Saxon jury. Not even one Frenchman. And a jury of only six.

CROWN

Our frontier ways are rough sometimes. A bit irregular. But—they get the job done.

> [DR. JUKES *and* DR. ROY *have come strolling
> from the left, similarly
> discussing the case.*]

JUKES

They'll hang him, doctor.

ROY

Is it so sure? You and I do not agree about him. So—the jury may not either.

JUKES

We shall soon know. Meanwhile, I've found him a most interesting patient. Forces me to re-examine my settled beliefs on many points.

ROY

It is like this, with the deranged. To work with them, it is to see how—what is your word—how—*precarious* is our hold on what we call sanity. What *is* sanity? To think of this—it can be frightening.

JUKES

Speaking of fright, I hate to imagine what *he's* going through now, poor devil. Sitting in there. . . .

ROY

Pardon. Kneeling. He prays. The jury considers, and he prays. He does not stop. He prays in French. In Latin. Mostly French. But sometimes in English! To make quite sure they will understand [*looking upward*] up there! But, I think it is all right, up there. I think *they* know some French!

JUKES

Unless, up there, they've quite lost touch with the French! Quite given them up.

ROY

Ah oui! And heaven now—full only of the English! This would be heaven!

JUKES

This levity, doctor. . . .

ROY

M'm! Not—English.

JUKES

Well, a trifle heartless, perhaps. With prisoner in there, bracing himself for the verdict. Guilty? Not guilty? Must be absolutely agonizing.

> [*They are now joined by the* CROWN
> *and the* DEFENCE.]

ROY

I think he genuinely believes his Saints will save him.

JUKES

Certainly if faith—utter faith could sway a verdict. . . .

CROWN

A court of law's a most unfavourable climate for miracles of faith.

DEFENCE

Even the faith of a prophet.

JUKES

Which reminds me—if it won't strike you as blasphe-
mous, gentlemen—I've been thinking we know a little
more now, of the considerations Pilate had to weigh—
in a case with, shall we say, certain parallels.

CROWN

[*But lightly, smiling.*] Doctor I consider that remark
one of the truest examples of profanity I've heard in
a long time.

JUKES

But some truth in it, don't you think? And in that particular connection, gentlemen, isn't it striking how
anxious the prisoner is to identify his own predicament
with the—Easter tragedy?

DEFENCE

That cross with himself hanging on it.

CROWN

Passion for martyrdom.

DEFENCE

Part of my case for him.

JUKES

Well, he may soon have what his heart desires. Jury
may be ready. Shall we go in?

[*They all go off right. As they are going, two
newspapermen come from the left and cross
to the right on their way back into the Court.*]

MARC

I'm *New York Times*. And you?

BILL

Aw, I'm just on the local. Case sure is getting cover-
age. World-wide!

MARC

Whole thing — Riel himself — newsman's answer to
prayer.

BILL

Sure is. Say what do the boys at the hotel think of his
chances now?

MARC

Odds this morning were he'd hang.

BILL

That's where I put my money too.

MARC

And me.

BILL

My little all.

MARC

First bet I ever hoped I'd lose.

BILL

Aw, I dunno. But I get you: Guy don't hang, if we lose. Kinda blood-money if we win.

MARC

You got it!

[They go off, right.]

SCENE 11 *Courtroom, Regina*

Court assembled as before.

CLERK
> Foreman of the jury.

> > [*The* FOREMAN *rises and bows, and*
> > *remains standing.*]

CLERK
> Are the jury agreed upon their verdict?

FOREMAN
> They are.

CLERK
> How say you: Is the prisoner guilty or not guilty?

FOREMAN
> Guilty.

CLERK
> Look to your verdict as the Court records it. You find the prisoner, Louis Riel, guilty—so say you all?

FOREMAN
> We do. [*He turns to Judge.*] Your Honour, there's something more.

JUDGE
> What is it?

FOREMAN
> I've been asked by my brother jurors to recommend the prisoner to the mercy of the Crown.

JUDGE

Your recommendation will be conveyed to the proper authorities. Thank you.

[*The* FOREMAN *bows and sits down.*]

JUDGE

Louis Riel, you have been found guilty of a crime the most pernicious that man can commit. You have been found guilty of high treason. For what you did your remarks form no excuse whatsoever, and the law requires you to answer for it. It's true, the jury have asked that Her Majesty give your case merciful consideration, but I can't hold out any hope that Her Majesty will open her hand in clemency to you. As for me, I have only one more duty to perform: that is, to tell you what the sentence of the law is upon you. All I can suggest or advise you is to prepare to meet your end.

[RIEL *clasps his hands before his breast and bows his head for the blow. The* JUDGE *puts on the black cap.*]

JUDGE

It is now my painful duty to pass sentence upon you, and that is, that you be taken now to the police guardroom at Regina, and that you be kept there till the eighteenth September next, and that you then be taken to the place appointed for your execution, and there be hanged by the neck till you are dead. And may God have mercy on your soul.

[*Spot one, out, on the Judge, leaving only Riel spot-lighted. For an intense, silent moment Riel stands motionless.*]

RIEL

[*Then, incredulous.*] St. Joseph! [*Then a cry of anguish.*] "St. Joseph!"

SCENE 12   *Corridor to Cells in Police Barracks, Regina*

JUKES *and the* POLICEMAN *are conversing anxiously and quietly.*

JUKES

How is it with him now?

POLICEMAN

Sometimes he's calm and studiously polite. But sometimes he starts up in a sort of wild delirium, painful to witness. He seems to see people crowding his cell, and to hear voices calling to him, mocking or deriding him.

JUKES

Phantoms. Phantom voices. Hallucinations.

POLICEMAN

But real, terribly real to him. It's as if all he's been through were flooding back, swamping his mind, till I fear for his reason, or what's left of it. [*A thumping is heard, accompanied by soft cries of lament: "Oh! Oh! Oh!"*] There, now! Pounding on the table with his fists and crying to himself—that terrible whimpering cry. . . .

JUKES

Yes, yes it's pitiful, pitiful.

POLICEMAN

Like an animal, trapped.

JUKES

I must observe this. I'll watch through the grid.

[JUKES *and the* POLICEMAN *go off, left.*]

SCENE 13 *Cell in Police Barracks, Regina*

Phantom tom-toms and mob-singing of "We'll hang him up the river" are heard, at first faintly, but coming up a little as light gradually comes up on RIEL. *He is revealed with his arms out and his fists clenched over the small table, almost identical with his position when seen waiting for the volley of the firing-squad at the execution of Thomas Scott. He thumps the table and cries, "Oh! Oh! Oh!" Phantom tom-toms and mob-singing now fade gradually out behind what follows.* RIEL *clutches the small metal statue of St. Joseph which stands on the table.*

RIEL

Oh St. Joseph, St. Joseph you promised me, you can not fail me. Help me. Help me, now. Pray for me. Mercy.

PHANTOM VOICE OF THE JUDGE

And may God have mercy on your soul.

RIEL

Mercy on my soul! Mercy on my soul! [*He looks round apprehensively, and starts up, as if he could see the priest. He picks up and carries, over one arm, the ball of the ball-and-chain shackle fastened to his ankle.*] Père André! Oh Père André, help me.

PHANTOM VOICE OF ANDRE

Our blessed Lady will protect you, pray to her.

Oh Mary ever blessed pray for me. Cover me. Hide
me. [*Complete change of tone and attitude as he thinks
he sees the Judge.*] Honourable Judge why are you
wearing the black cap? [*Crescendo to angry outburst.*]
Can all the people be guilty? A whole people guilty of
treason? Build scaffolds for them all! Make every tree
in The Saskatchewan a scaffold and hang us all, all, all
by the neck till we are dead, dead, dead and rotten
and our rotting corpses make a stench to fill the world.
. . . [*Ironic and bitter.*] And fill the noses of fine gentlemen sitting oh so pleased with themselves in Ottawa.

PHANTOM VOICES OF METIS

Louis Riel! Louis Riel!

RIEL

My Métis call me.

PHANTOM VOICE OF MOTHER

Louis my son, Louis!

RIEL

Maman! Maman! They called us savages! A little different tincture in the blood—savages! We own this
land! [*A new vision exalts him.*] Look, look, the herds
of buffalo, thundering across the plains! The men are
riding! [*He moves with their motion as if he saw
them.*] Pemmican! There will be lots of pemmican and
bonfires on the snow and pipes to smoke and singing
by the fires. The spring is on the plains! The sun is
strong, strong and rising high. Dance! Dance Métis,
dance! [*He claps his hands and sways, and his feet
make small motions in time with the dance.*] Eeeeee!
Dance, Indians, dance with us! Swing the coloured
feathers! Eeeeee! The anklets of angora and the tink-
ling bells make clouds about your feet! Dance! Dance!

[*His rhapsody is cut dead by
another phantom voice.*]

PHANTOM VOICE OF SCOTT

Riel!

RIEL

[*Horrified.*] Scott! Thomas Scott!

PHANTOM VOICE OF SCOTT

You'll hang for this!

[*The volley of the firing-squad is heard far off.*]

RIEL

Me too! Me too! My life too. . . . Oh there is blood, and blood!

[*Far off, a solemn bell slowly tolls three strokes.*]

RIEL

[After first stroke.] The bell.

VOICE AS OF ECHO

Riel.

RIEL

[*After the second stroke.*] The passing bell!

VOICE AS OF ECHO

Riel.

RIEL

[*After the third stroke.*] Not for Riel.

VOICE AS OF ECHO

Riel.

RIEL

No! No! Not for Riel! Turn back! Bid them turn back! I have a mission. I say I have a mission. God is with us. The Church is with us! His Grace has brought an amnesty. None will be punished. [*Derisive phantom laughter stops him. He pauses. Then, slow and grave.*] And immediately the cock crew! [*Pause.*] Who has betrayed Riel? They're in our streets! The redcoats riot in our streets, the drunken redcoats, where our young men and girls were dancing. [*The light begins to dim out.*] Dark. Dark. Everywhere. Fall rain! Fall! Black rain and darkness . . . fall on the redcoats . . . on Macdonald's redcoats . . . on the tents of Wolseley. [*Sinking down.*] Oh St. Joseph, hide me, shelter me, pray for me, now and in the hour of death. . . .

SCENE 14 *Precincts of Parliament, Ottawa*

An excited anti-Riel mob from Ontario demonstrates, down right. A similar pro-Riel demonstration from Quebec is down left. Light comes up first on the Ontario demonstrators. They shout, wave sticks, shake fists, wave flags. Roughly painted on boards that are hoisted on poles are legends and slogans which are also being shouted.

Death to Riel!
Vengeance for Thomas Scott!
Hang the traitor!
Hang Riel!
Hang Riel!
Hang Riel!

As light dims out on this Ontario mob it simultaneously comes up on the mob from Quebec.

Sursis Riel!
Vive Riel!
Reprieve!
Sursis!
Reprieve!
Reprieve!

SCENE 15 *Prime Minister's Room, Ottawa*

Sir John A. Macdonald, now seventy years old, sits at a table with the Honourable J. A. Chapleau, who is forty-three years old. Numerous press cuttings and reports are scattered on the table. There is a tray with whiskey and soda. Both men have drinks. Demonstrators in the previous scene are still heard, but now at a distance and dying out behind the discussion. Macdonald rises, with his glass, crosses and stands a moment listening.

MACDONALD

Hang! Reprieve! Hang! Reprieve! [*He returns to his seat.*] Oh hang the whole confounded boiling of them!

CHAPLEAU

It is not a comfortable position: horns of a dilemma!

MACDONALD

It's the very dickens of a position. But as we must somehow resolve the dilemma, let's examine the horns. Suppose the fellow hangs.

CHAPLEAU

If he hangs, Quebec revolts.

MACDONALD

Aye, every flag in Quebec will fly half-mast for him; and we may march behind his hearse into the wilderness perhaps for generations. R.I.P. Riel, R.I.P. Conservative Party. *And,* my dear Chapleau. [*A really important consideration.*] R.I.P. your political career, never to speak of my own.

CHAPLEAU

[*Smiling.*] You *do* regard it seriously, Sir John.

MACDONALD

Aye: what with this bawling for clemency—petitions, petitions, petitions, pleas, demands, threats—your entire French Catholic population, priests, people, press [*He tosses a handful of clippings.*] backed up by all the hysterical and sentimental public blatherers in the press of New York, Boston, Washington, Dublin, London, and even Paris and God alone knows where else besides—all determined, by a sort of inverted lynch law, to see that he doesn't hang.

CHAPLEAU

It demonstrates again the widespread revulsion, especially in America, against capital punishment for what is regarded as a political offence.

MACDONALD

A political *offence,* if we hang Riel, but a political *necessity,* when Riel shot Thomas Scott. An obliging sort of logic. [*Struck by something. Then, slyly.*] By the way, why *must* people associate the trial of Riel with the shooting of Thomas Scott.

CHAPLEAU

A most *dis*obliging sort of logic.

MACDONALD

However, if we take our cue from Quebec and *don't* hang him. . . .

CHAPLEAU

Then, of course, Ontario revolts.

MACDONALD

Ontario votes against us to an Orangeman. And we're back where we started from.

CHAPLEAU

You were so kind as to mention my personal career: I can't hide from myself that if we hang Riel, Quebec will print my signature to the death warrant side-by-side with the speeches I made in defence of his Adjutant, Ambroise Lépine, in the North-West ten years ago. Ah, those magnificent, impassioned speeches! Unfortunately, they would serve equally well in defence of Riel today.

MACDONALD

My dear Chapleau, don't start worrying about your former speeches. Any politician who does that is already among the damned, and he'll be the chief and probably the only mourner at his own funeral before he can say Jack Robinson. [*Struck by something associated with the name.*] Robinson, Henderson. Jack Henderson. [*Having got it.*] Och aye. Chapleau—by another pleasant little masterstroke of irony—the hangman at Regina is to be one, Jack Henderson—a former chum of the late lamented Thomas Scott at Fort Garry. I understand he actually applied—[*Mischievously.*] and to your brother the Sheriff out there—for the privilege, and I'm sure pleasure, of officiating.

CHAPLEAU

How the shade of Thomas Scott will laugh!

MACDONALD

An ugly laugh that will echo around Ontario and go cackling at Quebec till the very mischief is let loose.

CHAPLEAU

Assuming the execution. Are we now, in default of reason, being [*Slyly.*] "led to a decision" following our noses?

MACDONALD

[*His hand to his large nose.*] At least you and I have noses to follow: sound, reliable noses.

CHAPLEAU

Important part of a politician's equipment. Too often his only equipment.

MACDONALD

Unconscionably cynical remark, and I deplore cynicism—at any rate in my younger colleagues. However, while we indulge in these pleasantries, the impasse remains. Hang? Reprieve? One way or the other we must now decide and advise Her Majesty.

CHAPLEAU

If Whitehall would make the decision and save us the embarrassment.

MACDONALD

What else is Whitehall for? However, this time, Her Majesty's Imperial Government flatly refuses to play catspaw for us. Most inconsiderate of them. But this time we must risk burning our own paws—or should I say boats? No, my dear Chapleau, this wretch Riel is actually forcing us to take responsibility and govern Canada. How odd! The outlaw once more shapes the law. Henceforth, Louis Riel's name is scribbled across a chapter of our Constitutional Law! [*Offhand.*] However he's a gone coon.

CHAPLEAU

You are resolved?

MACDONALD

Live or die his miserable existence is nothing compared to what's endangered by it. I will hang or reprieve or do anything else that may be needed to prevent an unfortunate accident—his latest revolt— from fatally marring everything Confederation may mean—for Canada. And that is for the British Empire also, and the U.S.A., in short, for the world. When all has been considered and weighed, I think, perhaps, the public good will best be served if he hangs. There has been postponement already, of the date of execution. If you agree with me. . . .

CHAPLEAU

I do.

MACDONALD

Then we will advise no further interference with the judgment of the Court. I'm sure the Cabinet will concur.

CHAPLEAU

I feel relieved. His death at least removes an endless menace and anxiety.

MACDONALD

And he goes down to history as [*Ironically, slightly burlesque and pompous.*] one of the mortal instruments that shaped our destiny!

CHAPLEAU

As your hymn says, "God moves in a mysterious way. . . ."

MACDONALD

And so, I may add, does Satan. [*He holds up his glass of whiskey. For a moment stares through it meditatively. Then he speaks offhand and rather irritably.*] The execution will take place at Regina on November sixteen at eight o'clock in the morning. [*Swallows his whiskey at a gulp and puts down the glass.*]

SCENE 16   *Precincts of Police Barracks, Regina*

POLICEMAN, *officer of the North-West Mounted Police, already met, gazes across the barrack precincts to the plains.*

POLICEMAN

[*To himself.*] At eight he dies. Cold. Very cold. Snow everywhere. [*Pause.*] Now the sun. Gorgeous. Last dawn for Louis Riel. No attempt at rescue—yet. No sign of Gabriel Dumont. Any attempt by him—more than Riel will die. Our scouts—everywhere. The white houses of Regina, bright in the sun. People coming across the plains. So many, coming. On foot. Horseback. [*Sleighbells are heard.*] Buckboards, buggies, democrats, sleighs. All sorts of people. French. Indians. Settlers. Some—here from thousands of miles. Montreal. Toronto. Ottawa. Winnipeg. From across the Rockies. From British Columbia, even. And the U.S.A. [*Pause.*] Halted now. Our scouts, wheeling their horses across the trails. Thus far, good people! They're kneeling. Kneeling in the snow. Praying. Telling their beads. Some weep. Strange, very strange, this dawn on the prairies. Faces, all staring. Turned to stone. Staring toward this—"place appointed." Riel—quiet now. Waiting. His last hour. Last minutes. Quiet. [*Not reciting it.*] ". . Seas are quiet when the winds give o'er;
So calm are we when passions are no more.
For then we know how vain it was. . . . "

[*He is abruptly interrupted by a shouted command.*]

[*From somewhere fairly near by.*]

Leading section, right!
Form—half-sections!
Rear—halt!
Half-section—right!
Halt!
Eyes—right!
Dress!
Eyes—front!

SCENE 17   *Cell and Precincts in Police Barracks, Regina*

Light first picks up a small group, down left, waiting, as at one entrance to the cell. Nearest this imaginary entrance is the POLICEMAN. *Deputy* SHERIFF GIBSON, JUKES *and pressmen* MARC *and* BILL *are there. From the still unlighted area, mid-stage, comes a low murmur of voices—*ANDRE *and* RIEL, *reciting the creed. They continue in this throughout what the* SHERIFF *is saying.*

SHERIFF

[*Covering his agitation with an air of a brisk and business-like manner. He looks at his watch.*] What we've arranged: Last thing, when prisoner's on the drop and pinioned, all set, Father André will have him say the Lord's Prayer. At the words "And forgive us our trespasses"—oops! that's it! [*He snaps fingers and gestures.*] Alors, allez au ciel! I've rehearsed it with hangman Henderson. Whole thing should go off without a hitch. Oh! [*Grins.*] Hitch. No pun intended. [*Nervous laugh in which the others do not join.*]

[*The light remains on the Sheriff's group; now the mid-stage area, the interior of cell, is also lighted.* RIEL *is seen facing* ANDRE, *both kneeling. Another priest,* FATHER MCWILLIAMS, *stands up-stage from them holding a processional crucifix.* RIEL *and* ANDRE *have reached the last phrases of the creed.*]

RIEL *and* ANDRE

. . . The communion of Saints; the forgiveness of sins; the resurrection of the body; and life everlasting. Amen.

ANDRE

Rise, my son.

[*They rise.*]

RIEL

Resurrection. The resurrection of the body.

ANDRE

The time draws near.

RIEL

I have been given a fine morning—fine frosty morning.
I have loved such mornings on the plains.

ANDRE

It is a special favour that you have been given cheer-
fulness to meet this morning.

RIEL

God is with me.

ANDRE

The time is near. If there is any last thing you wish to
tell me.

RIEL

I had a vision, father. Three persons stood before me.
My brother, and a priest. And one I did not know, a
divine being. He pointed to me and said: "God will be
with him. They will destroy his body but God will
raise him up on the third day."

ANDRE

[*Embarrassed.*] My son, my son!

RIEL

[*Elated.*] For this my heart leaps up! I laugh! I go
with joy! The scaffold waits and I go gladly to it!
Happy to die! Oh do not fear. I shall not shame my
friends nor please my foes by failing at the end! I
shall not die a coward!

ANDRE

Your faith will support you. And now is that all?

RIEL

One last thing. I have one last thing to ask.

ANDRE

[*Being patient.*] What is it?

RIEL

On the scaffold, before I go, may I speak—some last
words?

ANDRE

To whom?

RIEL

To my people.

ANDRE

About what?

RIEL

About what I have done. What they should go on to do.

ANDRE

My son I beg you do not ask this.

RIEL

But father. . . .

ANDRE

No. Nothing is proper now but prayer—and silence.

RIEL

I have this right. If I must sacrifice it, too. . . . If it is required of me. . . .

ANDRE

I ask it of you. Your final sacrifice. In spirit you have already passed beyond these earthly things. Do not turn back, my son.

RIEL

[*Submissive.*] Oui, mon père, oui.

ANDRE

And now, are you at peace with all men?

RIEL

I am, father.

ANDRE

Do you forgive your enemies?

RIEL

I do.

ANDRE

Do you give your life a sacrifice to God?

RIEL

To God and my people, my half-breed people.

ANDRE

My son, I give you the kiss of peace.

[*He embraces* RIEL *and kisses him, first on one cheek,
then on the other. He holds the crucifix he carries
before* RIEL, *who kisses it and gazes at it. Somewhere
a clock begins to strike the hour. Down left—the
entrance to the cell—the* SHERIFF *comes to attention.*]

SHERIFF

Eight o'clock. Now. [*He turns and walks toward his
prisoner, the* POLICEMAN *standing aside to let him pass.*
JUKES *and the* PRESSMEN *remain behind. The* SHERIFF
halts beside RIEL *and* ANDRE.] It is the time. Are you
ready?

ANDRE

We are.

SHERIFF

As Sheriff I'll lead the way.

[*He moves toward the area down left. In procession
behind him follow* FATHER MCWILLIAMS *with the processional crucifix held aloft, then* ANDRE *and* RIEL. *At
down left, the procession turns and crosses the stage
slowly, down front to down right. At down left,* JUKES,
the POLICEMAN, *and the two* PRESSMEN *will fall in
behind* ANDRE *and* RIEL. *From the first steps of this
procession* ANDRE *recites the Confiteor and* RIEL
repeats it after him as they go forward.]

ANDRE

I confess to Almighty God. . . .

RIEL

I confess to Almighty God. . . .

ANDRE

To the blessed Mary ever Virgin. . . .

RIEL

To the blessed Mary ever Virgin. . . .

ANDRE

To blessed Michael the Archangel. . . .

RIEL

To blessed Michael the Archangel. . . .

ANDRE

To blessed John the Baptist. . . .

RIEL

To blessed John the Baptist. . . .

ANDRE

To the Holy Apostles Peter and Paul. . . .

RIEL

To the Holy Apostles Peter and Paul. . . .

ANDRE

And to all the Saints. . . .

RIEL

And to all the Saints. . . .

[*When* ANDRE *and* RIEL *are approaching the corner
down right, a bright light from off stage, up left,
catches in its beam the* HANGMAN, *who stands, black-
hooded and black-gauntleted, waiting to receive* RIEL
*and lead him off into the light—to the place where
the scaffold presumably is.*]

ANDRE

That I have sinned exceedingly in thought word and
deed. . . .

RIEL

That I have sinned exceedingly in thought word and
deed. . . .

ANDRE

Through my fault, through my fault, through my most
grievous fault. . . .

RIEL

Through my fault, through my fault, through my most
grievous fault. . . .

[*Down right, the procession turns towards the place
where the* HANGMAN *waits, up left. The eyes of* ANDRE
and RIEL *are on the ground, so they do not as yet see
the* HANGMAN.]

ANDRE

Therefore I beseech the blessed Mary ever Virgin. . . .

RIEL

Therefore I beseech the blessed Mary ever Virgin. . . .

ANDRE

Blessed Michael the Archangel. . . .

RIEL

Blessed Michael the Archangel. . . .

ANDRE

Blessed John. . . .

[*He abruptly breaks off, having lifted his eyes and seen the* HANGMAN *for the first time. He is so affected that he pauses and utters a small cry of horror. For a moment he seems too distressed to be able to go on.* RIEL, *by contrast, remains calm and composed, he turns in grave sympathy to encourage* ANDRE.]

RIEL

Courage, mon père, courage!

[ANDRE *braces himself and goes on.*]

ANDRE

Blessed John the Baptist. . . .

RIEL

Blessed John the Baptist. . . .

ANDRE

The Holy Apostles Peter and Paul. . . .

RIEL

The Holy Apostles Peter and Paul. . . .

ANDRE

And all the Saints. . . .

RIEL

And all the Saints. . . .

ANDRE

To pray to the Lord our God for me. . . .

RIEL

To pray to the Lord our God for me. . . .

[*While the procession is moving off into the light, up left the* HANGMAN *turns and walks alongside* RIEL *and upstage of him, with his gauntleted hand on* RIEL'*s shoulder. As they go on, a police* TROOPER—*off duty, tunic unbuttoned, smoking a cheroot, abristle with hostility—strolls in from up right and follows, slowly, to mid-stage, where he stands sardonically watching the procession as it passes out of sight repeating the last phrases of the Confiteor.*]

ANDRE

And may the Almighty God have mercy upon us. . . .

RIEL

And may the Almighty God have mercy upon us. . . .

ANDRE

And forgive us our sins. . . .

RIEL

And forgive us our sins. . . .

ANDRE

And bring us to life everlasting. . . .

RIEL

And bring us to life everlasting. . . .

ANDRE

Amen.

RIEL

Amen.

> [*In silence the* TROOPER *remains a moment gazing toward the light, which has begun to dim. Then:*]

TROOPER

[*Hoarse with hatred.*] Son of a bitch! [*He spits contemptuously after the procession. Then he throws down his cheroot and savagely grinds it underfoot.*] Goddam son of a bitch!

> [*He lurches off left.*]

SCENE 18   *A Place of Prayer and Mourning*

*A solemn bell tolls slowly and continues throughout
what follows to the end of the play. Simultaneously,
in* the distance, *mob voices may be heard jubilantly
singing "We'll hang him up the river" but with the
words changed to "He's hanging up the river." This
distant singing should only be heard during the first
eight strokes of the tolling bell—while* MOURNERS *are
assembling—and should fade out behind the opening
phrases of the requiem, leaving what remains of the
play to the serenity of last things. Meanwhile, from
down right and down left, Riel's* MOTHER *and*
MARGUERITE *and* PEOPLE *come in and, in a sort of ritual
movement, take their places and kneel in a semi-circle
with their backs to the audience. They kneel around*
ANDRE *who is at centre, with* FATHER MCWILLIAMS *a
pace upstage of him holding aloft a crucifix. At the
seventh stroke of the tolling bell—there should be an
interval of five seconds between successive strokes—
an off-stage male quartet begins to sing a four-part
unaccompanied requiem in Latin.*

OFF-STAGE MALE QUARTET

Requiem aeternam dona eis Domine et
lux perpetua luceat eis. In memoria aeterna erit
justus ab auditione mala non timebit.

> *[At the words "In memoria aeterna erit
> justus . . .",* ANDRE *accompanies the quartet,
> speaking the prayer in Latin or in
> English, but preferably in Latin.]*

ANDRE

Fac, quaesumus
Domine, hanc cum
servo tuo defuncto
misericordiam, ut
factorum suorum in
poenis non recipiat
vicem, qui tuam
in votis tenuit
voluntatem; ut sicut
hic cum vera fides
junxit fidelium
turmis, ita illic cum
tua miseratio societ
Angelicis choris.
Per Christum
Dominum nostrum.

[*Or*]

Grant, O Lord,
this mercy to Thy
servant departed;
that he who in his
desires did Thy will
may not receive the
punishments of his
misdeeds: and that
as true faith hath joined
him to the company of
the faithful here below,
Thy mercy may make
him the companion of
the holy Angels in
heaven. Through
Christ our Lord.

ALL

Amen.

[*The bell continues to toll.*]